tofu

tofu

making the most of this low-fat high-protein ingredient, with over 60 deliciously varied recipes from around the world

becky johnson

southwater

This edition is published by Southwater

Southwater is an imprint of Anness Publishing Ltd
Hermes House, 88–89 Blackfriars Road, London SE1 8HA
tel. 020 7401 2077; fax 020 7633 9499
www.southwaterbooks.com; info@anness.com

© Anness Publishing Ltd 2003, 2005

UK agent: The Manning Partnership Ltd, 6 The Old Dairy, Melcombe Road, Bath BA2 3LR
tel. 01225 478444; fax 01225 478440; sales@manning-partnership.co.uk

UK distributor: Grantham Book Services Ltd, Isaac Newton Way, Alma Park Industrial Estate, Grantham, Lincs NG31 9SD
tel. 01476 541080; fax 01476 541061; orders@gbs.tbs-ltd.co.uk

North American agent/distributor: National Book Network, 4501 Forbes Boulevard, Suite 200, Lanham, MD 20706
tel. 301 459 3366; fax 301 429 5746; www.nbnbooks.com

Australian agent/distributor: Pan Macmillan Australia, Level 18, St Martins Tower, 31 Market St, Sydney, NSW 2000
tel. 1300 135 113; fax 1300 135 103; customer.service@macmillan.com.au

New Zealand agent/distributor: David Bateman Ltd, 30 Tarndale Grove, Off Bush Road, Albany, Auckland
tel. (09) 415 7664; fax (09) 415 8892

A CIP catalogue record for this book is available from the British Library.

Publisher: Joanna Lorenz
Managing Editor: Linda Fraser
Editor: Jennifer Schofield
Editorial Reader: Jay Thundercliffe
Production Controller: Darren Price
Designer: Nigel Partridge
Indexer: Hilary Bird
Recipes: Matthew Drennen, Yasuko Fukuoka, Nicola Graimes, Kathy Man, Sallie Morris, Deh-Ta Hsuing
Photographers: Tim Auty, Martin Brigdale, Nicky Dowey, Michelle Garrett, Amanda Heywood,
Janine Hosegood, William Lingwood, Tom Odulate, Craig Robertson.

Previously published as *The Tofu Cookbook*

1 3 5 7 9 10 8 6 4 2

NOTES
Bracketed terms are intended for American readers.

For all recipes, quantities are given in both metric and imperial measures and, where appropriate, in standard cups and spoons.
Follow one set, but not a mixture, because they are not interchangeable.

Standard spoon and cup measures are level. 1 tsp = 5ml, 1 tbsp = 15ml, 1 cup = 250ml/8fl oz.

Australian standard tablespoons are 20ml. Australian readers should use 3 tsp
in place of 1 tbsp for measuring small quantities of gelatine, flour, salt, etc.

Medium (US large) eggs are used unless otherwise stated.

Main front cover image shows sweet-and-sour vegetables with tofu – for recipe, see page 54.

CONTENTS

INTRODUCTION

Although it is best known in the West by its Japanese name, tofu actually originated in China around 200 BC and was not introduced to Japan until the 8th century AD. Soya beans have been cultivated in China for thousands of years and many by-products from this valuable legume still constitute an important part of the Chinese diet. However, exactly how cooks developed the technique for making tofu, or bean curd as it is also known, is lost in the mists of the past.

Tofu was originally the food of Chinese aristocrats, noblemen and monks – indeed, it was Buddhist priests who first took Mongolian *doufu* to Japan during the Tang dynasty. Eating it was thought to promote longevity, a much prized virtue in traditional Chinese philosophy, and these elite classes certainly did live the longest. By the 16th century, the population at large had adopted tofu into their diet and by the late 1700s, tofu cookbooks had become increasingly popular.

Different types of tofu have been developed over the centuries. The Japanese were quick to create more refined forms of tofu, as well as inventing other soya products that matched the subtlety and delicacy of their cuisine. In China and Japan today, tofu is one of the most commonly used cooking ingredients.

Below: Clockwise from front left: soft or silken tofu, lightly seared tofu and firm tofu.

Until the twentieth century tofu had only been sampled by Westerners who had travelled to China and Japan. It remained a mere foreign curiosity until the early 1900s when the methods and techniques for tofu manufacture were introduced into Europe. From then on, tofu was made and used in the West. As the numbers of vegetarians and vegans increased, tofu, in all its forms, became more widely available, migrating from a few specialist health-food stores to

Above: Soya products contain isoflavones that are thought to lower cholesterol levels.

many mainstream supermarkets. Modern health concerns about cholesterol levels, obesity and dietary links with illnesses, such as cancers and heart disease, have stimulated people to seek healthy foodstuffs. Tofu contains isoflavones which are thought to lower cholesterol levels. More and more people are becoming aware of its health benefits as well as its great versatility in cooking.

Making tofu

The process of making tofu is a little like making soft cheese but much less time consuming. Soya beans are soaked, boiled, mashed and then sieved to produce soya "milk". Curds are then produced with the addition of a coagulant and, while warm, these are set in moulds for several hours. Finally, the tofu is released into a water tank to firm and cool further. When firm tofu is made, cotton cloths are laid across the base of the moulds to allow excess water to drain away. This often results in a distinctive cloth mark on the side of the tofu block. Silken tofu, on the other hand, is made with thicker soya milk and isn't drained.

Nutrition

Tofu and the closely related Indonesian tempeh are just two of the products that are made from the highly nutritious soya bean. The protein required by our bodies is made up of a number of amino acids and the protein found in soya beans provides amino acids that are closely aligned with the body's needs. Furthermore, because the manufacturing process removes the less digestible parts of the beans, our bodies can absorb 95 per cent of the protein present in tofu. Consequently, it is a good food for babies, the elderly and convalescents, as well as for vegans.

Tofu and soya bean products are high in linoleic acid, an unsaturated fatty acid that is effective in reducing blood cholesterol levels. They are also low in calories and have been proven to increase the amount of friendly bacteria

Below: Tofu is ideal for stir-fries, especially if you have time to marinate it first so that it can absorb a mixture of other flavours.

Above: The subtle flavour and soft texture of tofu means that it works well in all kinds of dishes.

in the gut so preventing constipation and reducing blood pressure. Soya bean products are high in isoflavones and several types of antioxidants, which help protect against and combat many serious diseases, including heart disease and some cancers. It is noteworthy that the increase in breast and prostate cancers is far lower in those countries with high soya consumption than in Britain and the United States, for example. Isoflavones, in combination with the high levels of calcium found in soya products, also help to maintain healthy bones and protect against osteoporosis. Also, tofu can help to relieve some of the symptoms associated with the menopause.

Cooking with tofu

Tofu is an incredibly adaptable ingredient and works well in most cuisines. It is best known in Chinese and Japanese food where it is eaten plain or marinated, coated in flour and deep-fried or roasted, added to fragrant soups or stir-fried. The subtle flavour and soft texture means that it can be added to all kinds of dishes without clashing with other ingredients. Tofu is also very sensitive to other flavours and is perfect for marinating, quickly becoming infused with a delicious depth of flavour. The

global vegetarian food culture has also seen an increasingly imaginative use of tofu, with chefs in California, London and Sydney developing recipes ranging from burgers to creamy dressings and sweet desserts. It also features in the cooking of the chefs of the relatively new Pacific Rim cuisine who innovatively marry flavours from East and West with thoroughly delectable results.

This book contains a wide collection of recipes that use tofu and other soya products. Although there is a predominance of recipes from Asia, these are balanced by Western recipes that illustrate tofu's adaptability.

While cooking with tofu, tempeh and other soya products is not difficult, there are ways of preparing and techniques for handling these products that help to guarantee successful results. The introductory section of this book gives a helpful survey of the types of soya products available and their uses, along with step-by-step instructions for all the essential preparation and cooking techniques, from pressing tofu to deep-frying, and offers advice on some of the more unusual treatments of this versatile ingredient.

Below: Tofu is particularly good in soups, combined with fresh vegetables.

TYPES of TOFU

There is a surprisingly large range of different kinds of tofu available, but you may have to go to a Chinese or Japanese food store to buy some of the less familiar ones. It's worth visiting an Asian supermarket in any case, even when buying the most common kinds of tofu, as high quality is virtually guaranteed.

Firm tofu

Also known as cotton-strained tofu because of the way it is made, this is the traditional Chinese tofu that is harder to crumble. It is shaped into firm blocks or cakes, measuring about 7.5cm/3in square and 2.5cm/1in thick. It is available fresh or in vacuum packs, which need to be drained before use. For best results, firm tofu should be pressed before use to remove the excess water.

Firm tofu can be cubed or sliced for use in stir-fries, on skewers or in casseroles, curries, soups and salads. Alternatively, it can be mashed and used in baked dishes and burgers. Firm tofu has a slightly grainy texture and needs gentle handling, as it will break into smaller pieces especially when cooked. To avoid this, you can blanch the pieces in boiling water or briefly fry them in oil to harden them before stir-frying or braising. Always use a sharp knife when slicing firm tofu, as a blunt blade will squash it and cause the tofu block to crumble.

Firm tofu is bland in flavour and should be used with ingredients that are flavoursome. It is also perfect

for marinating, as it has a porous nature that absorbs flavours quickly and easily.

Firm tofu that is vacuum-packed will keep for weeks in the refrigerator. Fresh firm tofu should be kept submerged in water in a plastic box in the refrigerator. Change the water daily and use the tofu within a week. Freezing is not recommended as this alters the texture of the tofu.

A lightly seared version, called *yaki-dofu* in Japan, is also available. It is used mainly in Japanese hot-pots.

Silken tofu

This is the original Japanese type of tofu, and is also known as silken-strained tofu. It has a finer texture than firm tofu and is available fresh and in long-life vacuum packs.

Silken tofu is soft and breaks down easily, so is best added at the last minute to soups or sprinkled over stir-fries or salads. However, it really comes into its own when used to make sauces, dips, salad dressings and sweet fools or

Left: Marinated tofu

whips, as it imparts a rich creamy texture and takes on intense flavours. In fact, it is the perfect low-fat alternative to cream, soft cheese, crème fraîche and yogurt and can be used as a substitute for dairy products in many recipes. This is especially useful to those people who are lactose intolerant and for vegans.

Fresh silken tofu should be stored in the refrigerator and used within one week. The vacuum-packed type does not need to be stored in the refrigerator. It should not be frozen.

Marinated tofu

Also known as pressed tofu, marinated tofu is made by compressing fresh tofu until almost all of the liquid has been squeezed out, leaving a solid block with a smooth texture. The tofu is then marinated in a mixture of soy sauce and Chinese five-spice powder, which colours the outside a rich dark brown, while the inside remains white. It is available in vacuum packs from Asian stores. and can also be bought from some health-food stores and supermarkets.

Marinated tofu offers a contrast in both texture and flavour when combined with other ingredients. It can be used in

Above: Clockwise from left: silken tofu, Japanese thin deep-fried tofu sheets, firm tofu and Japanese thick deep-fried tofu.

a similar way to firm tofu, shredded or cut into thin slices and stir-fried with meat and/or vegetables. Marinated tofu is also a good choice for kebabs and can be added to casseroles, soups and stews.

It will keep for several weeks in the refrigerator, in an airtight container. However, it should not be frozen.

Smoked tofu

Firm tofu is also available smoked, which adds a distinctive flavour. Some brands have added ingredients such as spices and herbs. It can be used in stir-fries and salads, and is also good in pasta and rice dishes. Smoked tofu will keep for up to one month in the refrigerator.

Frozen tofu

Freeze-dried, frozen tofu is different in every way from firm or silken tofu. It has a spongy texture and a rich flavour, even after soaking in water, and does not disintegrate however long it is cooked. The process of freezing and thawing is what produces its characteristic texture.

Frozen tofu is available from Japanese stores and is often sold in packets of five pieces together with a powdered soup stock in which to cook it. It may simply be called frozen tofu (or dofu) or labelled *koya-dofu* or *koguri-dofu*.

If you buy it in a pack with soup stock, it can be cooked to produce an almost instant meal. If the packet does not contain sachets of powdered soup, frozen tofu should be soaked in hot water for 5 minutes before cooking. Squeeze out the milky water a few times until it becomes clear. The tofu can then be simply eaten as it is or cooked with other ingredients. Typically it is simmered with vegetables and shiitake mushrooms in a rich soup or stew and is used for Buddhist monk's vegetarian cooking, known as *shojin ryori*.

Unopened packets of frozen tofu will keep for a long time, but check and do not exceed the "use by" date.

Above: Bean curd skins *are available from Japanese stores as flat sheets, rolled and cut, or in thick strips.*

Deep-fried tofu

Fairly tasteless, but with an interesting texture, this is fresh firm tofu that has been cut into cubes or triangles and deep-fried in vegetable oil until golden brown. There are both Japanese and Chinese versions of deep-fried tofu that differ very slightly, but may be used interchangeably. Deep-fried tofu is available from larger supermarkets and Asian stores. It is quite robust and does not disintegrate during cooking. To reduce the oiliness, rinse deep-fried tofu in boiling water and pat dry with kitchen paper before cooking.

When cooked, deep-fried tofu puffs up so that the golden, crisp coating becomes a somewhat baggy casing for the creamy white tofu inside. The coating readily absorbs flavours and makes it best suited to marinating in, dressing with or dipping into strong-flavoured sauces, especially those containing soy sauce and chilli. Deep-fried tofu is used in the same ways as firm tofu in soups, casseroles, stir-fries and braised dishes and features in some Japanese seaweed dishes. Japanese thin deep-fried tofu sheets can be slit open in the same way as pitta bread and stuffed with minced (ground) pork, chicken, fish or prawns (shrimp), then braised in a sauce. Japanese thick deep-fried tofu is fried as a whole block, so is only brown on the outside, while the inside remains white.

Deep-fried tofu does not keep well as it becomes soggy. It can be crisped again by baking, stir-frying or grilling (broiling). It can be frozen for up to one year.

OTHER SOYA BEAN PRODUCTS

Arguably, Japan produces the widest range of soya bean products, but China and other Asian countries are close behind.

Bean curd skins

These are made from soya "milk". A large pan of the milk is brought to the boil, then the thin layer of skin that forms on the surface is skimmed off with a stick in a single action and hung up to dry – a simple-sounding technique that requires considerable skill. When dry, the milk forms a flat sheet or skin. Bean curd skins should be soaked in water for 1–2 hours before cooking. Like fresh tofu, bean curd skins have little flavour and aroma of their own but readily absorb the flavours of other ingredients during cooking. The skins are used in stir-fries, soups and casseroles and, occasionally, as wrappers for spring rolls.

Store bean curd skins in their original packets or in a sealed plastic bag in a cool dry place, where they will keep well.

Above: Frozen tofu, known in Japan as koya-dofu, *is believed to have been invented by Buddhist monks on the Koya mountain many centuries ago.*

Left: Indonesian tempeh has a firmer, rougher texture than tofu.

Above: Cubed and minced (ground) textured vegetable protein.

Bean curd sticks

These are made in the same way as bean curd skins but when the skin is still warm, it is rolled up and left to dry.

Bean curd sticks require much longer soaking than the skins, and they should be soaked overnight. They have no taste of their own but will absorb the flavour of other ingredients. Bean curd skins can be chopped and added to a variety of vegetarian dishes and also cooked with meat in braised dishes and casseroles.

They should be stored in a sealed plastic bag in a cool and dry place.

Tempeh

Similar to tofu, but with a nuttier, more savoury flavour and firmer texture, tempeh is an Indonesian speciality. It is made by fermenting cooked soya beans with a culture. It is available chilled or frozen from health-food and Asian supermarkets.

Like firm tofu, tempeh benefits from marinating and can be used in many of the same ways – in stir-fries and kebabs, for example. However, its firmer texture also makes it an excellent meat rather than dairy substitute, so it is perfect in casseroles and baked dishes such as pies.

Chilled tempeh can be stored in the refrigerator for up to a week. Frozen tempeh can be stored in the freezer for a month and should be thawed completely before using.

Textured vegetable protein

This was specifically designed as a replacement for meat and is made from processed soya beans. Textured vegetable protein (TVP) is usually sold in dry chunks or minced (ground) and is widely available from Asian stores and large supermarkets.

TVP needs to be rehydrated with boiling water or stock before it is used in stews, curries or as a filling for pies. It readily absorbs the flavours of other ingredients, such as herbs and spices.

Stored in a cool, dry place, TVP will keep for a long time.

Soy sauce

The recipe for this traditional condiment has changed little in 2,000 years. It is made by combining crushed soya beans with wheat, salt, water and a yeast-based culture, which is then left to ferment for anything from six months to three years. This type of soy sauce is described as naturally brewed or fermented. There are also brands that are chemically prepared to speed up the fermentation process and these may contain additional flavourings and colourings. Not only are these vastly inferior in flavour to naturally brewed soy sauce, but they have also been the subject of health scares in recent years.

There are two basic types of soy sauce, light and dark. Light soy sauce is saltier and slightly thinner in consistency. It is used in dressings and soups and as a table condiment. Dark soy sauce is heavier, sweeter and has a more rounded flavour. It is used in marinades, stir-fries and sauces.

Soy sauce is widely available from supermarkets, but it is worth visiting Asian food stores for the brands that the Chinese use themselves. Once opened, store in the refrigerator.

Shoyu

This is the Japanese version of soy sauce. It is quite salty and has a very strong colour. It is aged for up to two years to

Above: Tamari (left) and shoyu – Japanese soy sauces.

SOYA DAIRY SUBSTITUTES

Soya "milk", "cream", "yogurt" and "cheese" are available from health-food stores and supermarkets and are ideal for vegans, people who prefer not to eat dairy products and anyone with a lactose intolerance.

Made from the pulverized beans, soya milk is the most widely used alternative to milk. It is slightly thicker than cow's milk and has a nutty flavour. It is suitable for both cooking and drinking and is used to make yogurt, cream and cheese substitutes.

Soya cream is made with a higher proportion of beans than the milk, so it has a richer flavour and thicker texture. It has a similar consistency to single (light) cream and can be used in the same ways.

Soya cheese is made from a blend of processed beans and vegetable fats and may be flavoured with herbs and spices. It can lack the depth of flavour of cheese made from cow's, goat's or sheep's milk, but may be used in the same ways. Store in the refrigerator.

Right: Soya milk products are ideal for vegans or people who have a lactose intolerance. Clockwise, from front: yogurt, cheese, milk and cream.

produce a mellow sauce that can be used as a dip on its own for sushi, but is also used in the same ways as Chinese dark soy sauce. Once the bottle has been opened, keep it in the refrigerator.

Tamari

This soy sauce, which is a natural by-product of miso production, is usually made without wheat, so it is ideal for people with a gluten intolerance. It has a rich, robust flavour and is used in cooking and as a table condiment. It should be stored in the refrigerator.

Miso

A thick paste, made from a mixture of cooked soya beans, rice, wheat or barley, salt and water, that is left to ferment for up to three years. Miso is available from large supermarkets.

It is used to add a savoury flavour to soups, stocks, stir-fries and noodle dishes. There are three strengths: white miso (called shiro-miso in Japanese) is the lightest and sweetest; medium miso (aka-miso in Japanese), preferred for everyday use, is mellow; and kuro-miso or dark miso has a thick texture and a strong flavour.

Miso keeps very well and can be stored, unopened, for several months. Keep open miso in the refrigerator.

Above: Medium miso (top) and dark miso (left). Miso is one of the oldest of Japanese ingredients – it was probably first made in the 12th century.

PREPARATION and COOKING TECHNIQUES

Tofu is very fragile and although the firm variety is more robust than silken tofu, both should be handled with care to prevent crumbling.

Pressing firm tofu

Silken tofu is usually used as it is, but firm tofu needs to be pressed before cooking to squeeze out any excess water. This process makes the block firmer on the outside, and therefore ideal for deep-frying and stir-fries.

1 Unpack the tofu block and discard the liquid. then wrap the tofu in three layers of kitchen paper or a tea towel. Alternatively, you could place the block of tofu on a slightly tilting chopping board and place a smaller board on top.

2 If wrapped, place a large plate on top of the tofu, so that the whole block is covered. Put a weight, such as a heavy book, on top of the plate or smaller chopping board.

3 Leave the tofu to press for up to 1 hour, until all the excess water has been absorbed or has run down the tilted board, and the block of tofu is about half its original weight. If wrapped, unwrap the tofu and pat dry with kitchen paper.

Searing firm tofu

Briefly searing the outside of firm tofu helps to prevent it from disintegrating during stir-frying.

1 Press the block of tofu for up to 1 hour to drain off the excess water.

2 Heat a griddle pan or heavy frying pan and brush with a little oil. When it is very hot, add the tofu and cook for a few seconds on each side, pressing it down gently in the pan. Remove the tofu from the pan.

Cutting firm tofu

Firm tofu can be cut into slices or cubes. Always use a sharp knife when handling tofu as a blunt knife will squash the tofu and cause it to crumble.

1 Once the excess water has been drained from the block of firm tofu. pat the tofu dry with a clean piece of kitchen paper.

2 Place the tofu on a clean chopping board and cut the block into slices about 2cm/¾in thick or the required size for the recipe. If the recipe calls for cubes, cut the slices in half, and, finally, into cubes.

Marinating firm tofu

Tofu is relatively tasteless but readily takes on other flavours. It is at its best when marinated in strongly flavoured seasonings, aromatic oils, soy sauce, spices or herbs.

Cut a block of tofu into 1cm/½in cubes and leave to marinate in a mixture of groundnut (peanut) oil, sesame oil, soy sauce, crushed garlic, grated fresh root ginger and honey for at least 1 hour.

MARINADES

These quantities are sufficient for about 225g/8oz firm tofu.

Chinese red marinade

45ml/3 tbsp dark soy sauce, 30ml/2 tbsp Chinese rice wine, 15ml/1 tbsp grated fresh root ginger, 1 crushed garlic clove, 10ml/2 tsp soft dark brown sugar, 2.5ml/½ tsp Chinese five-spice powder and a pinch of ground, roasted Sichuan peppercorns.

Fresh herb marinade

30ml/2 tbsp olive oil, 50ml/2fl oz dry white wine, 7.5ml/1½ tsp lemon juice and 15ml/1 tbsp chopped fresh herbs. Season with black pepper.

Spicy Indian marinade

½ finely chopped onion, 1 crushed garlic clove, 2.5ml/½ tsp grated fresh root ginger, 2.5ml/½ tsp ground cumin, 2.5ml/½ tsp ground coriander, 1.5ml/¼ tsp ground turmeric and 75ml/5 tbsp natural (plain) yogurt.

Pan-frying firm tofu

Firm tofu is given a crisp texture on the outside but remains soft on the inside if it is pan-fried. Frying firm tofu before using it, also helps to prevent it from crumbling or breaking.

1 Press a block of firm tofu to remove the excess liquid, then pat the block dry with kitchen paper. Slice the tofu into even-size cubes.

2 Preheat 30ml/2 tbsp groundnut (peanut) oil in a wok or large frying pan and fry the tofu for 4–5 minutes until golden brown, turning occasionally.

3 Use a slotted spoon to remove the cubes and set aside until needed.

Deep-frying firm tofu

For a lovely crisp texture, cubes of firm tofu can be deep-fried before combining them with other ingredients in a dish.

1 Press a block of firm tofu to drain off the excess liquid, then cut it into cubes.

2 Half-fill a wok with oil and heat to 180–190°C/350–375°F or until a cube of day-old bread browns in 30 seconds. Add the tofu cubes and deep-fry, turning once, for a few minutes, until light golden brown. Remove with a slotted spoon and drain on kitchen paper. Do not overcrowd the wok.

Processing silken tofu

Silken tofu does not need to be pressed and can be used straight from the packet.

Put the silken tofu into the bowl of a food processor or blender. Use a wooden spoon or the back of a fork to break the tofu into smaller pieces, then process or blend the tofu until it is at the required consistency for the recipe.

Preparing thin deep-fried tofu

Thin sheets of deep-fried tofu, called *abura-age*, are used in Japanese cooking.

1 Place the deep-fried tofu in a sieve and pour boiling water over them to wash off any excess oil. Drain off the water and pat dry with kitchen paper. Par-boil it in rapidly boiling water for 1 minute, then drain and leave to cool. Squeeze out any excess water.

2 Place the tofu sheets on a chopping board and cut each sheet in half.

3 Carefully pull each half sheet open by rubbing the outside back and forth with the palm of your hand to ease the sides apart. Use your fingers to open the bag fully, working your way carefully towards the bottom. If the bags are not opening easily, gently insert a round-bladed knife into the bag and work around the bag opening it out gradually.

Draining tempeh

Although it has a firmer texture than tofu, tempeh also benefits from draining.

Place the tempeh in a wire sieve set over a bowl and leave it to drain until the excess liquid has collected in the bowl. If using frozen tempeh, you can thaw and drain it simultaneously in the refrigerator or in a cool place.

Marinating tempeh

Although tempeh has a nuttier, more savoury flavour than tofu, it still benefits from marinating. Use a mixture of flavoured oils, aromatic ingredients and spices and leave for at least 1 hour.

Cutting tempeh

If you use a sharp knife, you should have no problems cutting tempeh into cubes.

Cut the tempeh into slices that are 1–2cm/½–¾in thick, then cut the slices in half and, finally, into cubes.

SOUPS AND APPETIZERS

Light, delicate and versatile, tofu is the perfect
choice for the first course as it stimulates the
appetite. Soups and appetizers should be a feast
for the eyes, too, and there is no shortage
of visual delights here – from the minimalist
elegance of Deep-fried Tofu in Dashi Soup to the
colourful abundance of Vegetable Salad with
Tahini Tofu Dressing.

HOT-and-SWEET VEGETABLE and TOFU SOUP

An interesting combination of hot, sweet and sour flavours that makes for a soothing, nutritious soup. It takes only minutes to make as the spinach leaves and silken tofu are simply placed in bowls and covered with the well-flavoured hot stock.

SERVES 4

1.2 litres/2 pints/5 cups vegetable stock
5–10ml/1–2 tsp Thai red curry paste
2 kaffir lime leaves, torn
40g/1½oz/3 tbsp palm sugar or light
    muscovado (brown) sugar
30ml/2 tbsp soy sauce
juice of 1 lime
1 carrot, cut into thin batons
50g/2oz baby spinach leaves, any coarse
    stalks removed
225g/8oz silken tofu, diced

1 Heat the stock in a large pan, then add the red curry paste. Stir constantly over a medium heat until the paste has dissolved. Add the lime leaves, sugar and soy sauce and bring to the boil.

2 Add the lime juice and carrot to the pan. Reduce the heat and simmer for 5–10 minutes. Place the spinach and tofu in four individual serving bowls and pour the hot stock on top to serve.

TOM YAM GUNG with TOFU

One of the most refreshing and healthy soups, this fragrant and colourful dish is a Thai speciality. It would make an ideal light lunch or supper on its own or could be served with a selection of several different dishes, in the Thai style.

SERVES 4

300g/11oz firm tofu
30ml/2 tbsp groundnut
    (peanut) oil
1.2 litres/2 pints/5 cups good
    vegetable stock
15ml/1 tbsp Thai chilli jam
grated rind of 1 kaffir lime
1 shallot, thinly sliced
1 garlic clove, finely chopped
2 kaffir lime leaves, shredded
3 red chillies, seeded and shredded
1 lemon grass stalk, finely chopped
6 shiitaki mushrooms, thinly sliced
4 spring onions (scallions), shredded
45ml/3 tbsp Thai fish sauce
45ml/3 tbsp lime juice
5ml/1 tsp caster (superfine) sugar
45ml/3 tbsp chopped fresh
    coriander (cilantro)
salt and ground black pepper

1 Wrap the tofu in kitchen paper and place a plate on top, so that the it covers the tofu. Put a weight on it and leave to press. Cut the tofu into bitesize pieces.

2 Heat the oil in a wok, add the tofu and cook over a medium heat, turning occasionally, for about 4–5 minutes, until golden. Use a slotted spoon to remove it and set aside. Tip the oil from the wok into a large heavy pan.

3 Add the stock, chilli jam, kaffir lime rind, shallot, garlic, lime leaves, two-thirds of the chillies and the lemon grass to the pan. Bring to the boil, lower the heat and simmer for 20 minutes.

4 Strain the stock into a clean pan. Stir in the remaining chilli, the shiitaki mushrooms, spring onions, Thai fish sauce, lime juice and sugar. Simmer for 3 minutes. Add the fried tofu and heat through for 1 minute. Mix in the chopped coriander and season to taste. Serve immediately in warmed bowls.

COOK'S TIP
Fresh kaffir limes and leaves are available from South-east Asian stores. If you cannot find them, use freeze dried leaves, which are widely available, or grated ordinary lime rind.

INDONESIAN TOFU LAKSA

*This spicy soup, with deep-fried tofu, is not a dish you can throw together in a few minutes,
but it is marvellous party food. Guests spoon noodles into wide soup bowls, add accompaniments
of their choice, top up with soup and then take a few prawn crackers to nibble.*

SERVES 6

675g/1½lb small clams
2 × 400ml/14fl oz cans coconut milk
50g/2oz ikan bilis (dried anchovies)
900ml/1½ pints/3¾ cups water
115g/4oz shallots, finely chopped
4 garlic cloves, chopped
6 macadamia nuts or blanched
    almonds, chopped
3 lemon grass stalks, root trimmed
90ml/6 tbsp sunflower oil
1cm/½in cube shrimp paste
25g/1oz/2 tbsp mild curry powder
a few curry leaves
2–3 aubergines (eggplant), total weight
    about 675g/1½lb, trimmed
675g/1½lb raw peeled prawns (shrimp)
10ml/2 tsp sugar
1 head Chinese leaves (Chinese cabbage),
    thinly sliced
115g/4oz/2 cups beansprouts, rinsed
2 spring onions (scallions), finely chopped
50g/2oz crispy fried onions
115g/4oz deep-fried tofu
675g/1½lb mixed noodles (laksa, mee and
    behoon) or one type only
prawn (shrimp) crackers, to serve

1 Scrub the clams under cold running water and then put them in a large pan with 1cm/½in water. Bring to the boil, cover and steam over a high heat for about 3–4 minutes, until all the clams have opened. Drain and discard any that remain shut. Make up the coconut milk to 1.2 litres/2 pints/5 cups with water. Put the ikan bilis (dried anchovies) in a pan and add the water. Bring to the boil and simmer for 20 minutes.

2 Meanwhile, put the shallots, garlic and nuts into a mortar. Cut off the lower 5cm/2in of two of the lemon grass stalks, chop finely and add to the mortar. Pound the mixture to a paste.

3 Heat the oil in a large heavy pan, add the shallot paste and cook, stirring constantly, for 1–2 minutes, until the mixture gives off a rich aroma. Bruise the remaining lemon grass stalk and add to the pan. Toss over the heat to release its flavour. Mix the shrimp paste and curry powder to a paste with a little of the coconut milk, add to the pan and toss the mixture over the heat for 1 minute, stirring constantly, and keeping the heat low. Stir in the remaining coconut milk. Add the curry leaves and leave the mixture to simmer gently while you prepare the accompaniments.

COOK'S TIP
Dried shrimp or prawn paste, also called blachan, is sold in small blocks and is available from Asian supermarkets.

4 Strain the stock into a pan. Discard the ikan bilis, bring to the boil, then add the aubergines. Cook for about 10 minutes, or until tender and the skins can be peeled off easily. Lift out of the stock, peel and cut into thick strips.

5 Arrange the aubergines on a serving platter. Sprinkle the prawns with sugar, add to the stock and cook for about 2–4 minutes, until they have just turned pink. Remove with a slotted spoon and place next to the aubergines. Add the Chinese leaves, beansprouts, spring onions and crispy fried onions to the platter, together with the clams.

6 Gradually stir the remaining ikan bilis stock into the pan of soup and bring to the boil. Rinse the fried tofu in boiling water, cool slightly and squeeze to remove excess oil. Cut each piece in half and add to the soup. Lower the heat to a very gentle simmer.

7 Cook the noodles according to the instructions of the packet, drain and pile in a dish. Remove the curry leaves and lemon grass from the soup and discard. Place the noodles, soup and the platter of seafood and vegetables on the table, along with a bowl of prawn crackers so that guests can then help themselves.

VARIATION
You could substitute mussels for clams if you like. Scrub them thoroughly, removing any beards, and cook them in lightly salted water for about 5 minutes, until they open. Like clams, discard any mussels that remain closed.

MINESTRONE with MARINATED FRIED TOFU

This satisfying and appealing soup is a meal in itself and can be adapted to use whatever vegetables are available. It is especially tasty if made with fresh seasonal produce but can also be made with frozen mixed vegetables.

SERVES 6

15ml/1 tbsp olive oil
2 leeks, finely chopped
2 celery sticks, finely diced
2 garlic cloves, finely chopped
2 courgettes (zucchini), finely diced
450g/1lb carrots, finely diced
200g/7oz green beans, finely sliced
5ml/1 tsp dried Mediterranean herbs
1.2 litres/2 pints/5 cups vegetable stock
400g/14oz can chopped tomatoes
300g/11oz marinated deep-fried
    tofu pieces
20g/¾oz bunch flat leaf parsley or
    basil, chopped
sea salt and ground black pepper

VARIATION
Marinated deep-fried tofu adds an extra dimension to the flavour, but could be replaced with cubed firm or silken tofu.

1 Preheat the oven to 200°C/400°F/ Gas 6. Heat the oil in a large pan then sauté the leeks, celery and garlic for 7–8 minutes, or until softened and beginning to turn golden.

2 Add the other vegetables and dried herbs. Stir to mix well, then pour over the vegetable stock and canned tomatoes. Bring to the boil, then simmer for 20–25 minutes, until the vegetables are tender.

3 Meanwhile, place the tofu pieces on a baking sheet and bake for 8–10 minutes to warm through.

4 Add the chopped parsley or basil to the soup and season to taste with sea salt and pepper. Stir in the warmed tofu and serve immediately sprinkled with a grinding of extra black pepper.

SHANGHAI TOFU SPRING ROLLS

It is said that these crisp snacks were traditionally served with tea when visitors came to call after the Chinese New Year. As this was springtime, they came to be known as spring rolls. Buy fresh or frozen spring roll wrappers from Asian stores.

MAKES 12

12 spring roll wrappers, thawed if frozen
30ml/2 tbsp plain (all-purpose) flour, mixed
    to a paste with water
sunflower oil, for deep-frying

For the filling
6 Chinese dried mushrooms, soaked for
    30 minutes in warm water
150g/5oz fresh firm tofu
30ml/2 tbsp sunflower oil
225g/8oz finely minced (ground) pork
225g/8oz peeled cooked prawns (shrimp),
    coarsely chopped
2.5ml/½ tsp cornflour (cornstarch), mixed
    to a paste with 15ml/1 tbsp light
    soy sauce
75g/3oz each shredded bamboo shoots or
    grated carrot, sliced water chestnuts
    and beansprouts
6 spring onions (scallions) or 1 young leek,
    finely chopped
a little sesame oil

For the dipping sauce
100ml/3½fl oz/scant ½ cup light soy sauce
15ml/1 tbsp chilli sauce
a little sesame oil
rice vinegar, to taste

1 To make the filling, drain the mushrooms. Cut off and discard the stems and slice the caps finely. Slice the tofu.

2 Heat the oil in a wok and stir-fry the pork for 2–3 minutes, or until the colour changes. Add the prawns, cornflour paste and bamboo shoot or carrot. Stir in the water chestnuts.

3 Increase the heat, add the beansprouts and spring onions or leek and toss for 1 minute. Stir in the mushrooms and tofu. Remove the wok from the heat, season, then stir in the sesame oil. Cool quickly on a large platter.

4 Separate the spring roll wrappers. Place a wrapper on the work surface with one corner nearest you. Spoon some of the filling near the centre of the wrapper and fold the nearest corner over the filling. Brush a little of the flour paste on the free sides, turn the sides into the middle and roll up the wrapper to enclose the filling. Repeat with the remaining wrappers and filling.

5 Deep-fry the spring rolls, in batches, in oil heated to 190°C/375°F until they are crisp and golden. Drain on kitchen paper and serve immediately with the dipping sauce, made by mixing all the ingredients in a bowl.

DEEP-FRIED TOFU in DASHI SOUP

A creamy tofu block is lightly dusted with flour, deep-fried in hot oil, then soaked in hot broth. This tasty, filling and aesthetically pleasing dish is typical in a shojin ryori (Zen vegetarian) menu, as practised by Buddhist monks in Japan.

SERVES 4

2 × 300g/11oz packets silken tofu
vegetable oil, for deep-frying
30ml/2 tbsp plain (all-purpose) flour

For the sauce
50ml/2fl oz/¼ cup shoyu
50ml/2fl oz/¼ cup mirin (sweet rice wine)
pinch of salt
300ml/½ pint/1¼ cups water and 7.5ml/
   1½ tsp dashi-no-moto (see Cook's Tip)

For the garnish
2.5cm/1in fresh root ginger, peeled and
   finely grated
60ml/4 tbsp finely chopped chives

COOK'S TIP
Dashi-no-moto is Japanese stock granules, available in Asian supermarkets.

1 Drain the water from the tofu. Carefully open the packet and then wrap the tofu in 2–3 layers of kitchen paper. Set a chopping board, or large plate with a weight, on top to press the tofu, and leave for at least 30 minutes for the excess liquid to be absorbed by the kitchen paper.

2 To make the sauce, place the shoyu, mirin, salt and dashi stock in a small pan over a medium heat. Mix well, cook for 5 minutes, then set aside.

3 Squeeze the grated ginger and make into four small balls. Set aside.

4 Unwrap the tofu and pat dry with another sheet of kitchen paper. Slice one tofu block into four squares each about 2.5 × 6cm/1 × 2½in. Repeat with the other tofu block.

5 Heat the oil to about 190°C/375°F. Dust the tofu with the flour and slide it into the oil. Deep-fry until golden brown. Drain well on kitchen paper.

6 Arrange two tofu pieces in each of four small bowls. Reheat the sauce and gently pour from the side of the bowl. Try not to splash over the tofu. Put a ginger ball on the tofu and sprinkle with chives. Serve hot.

STUFFED and GRILLED THIN TOFU

Age or abura-age (thin deep-fried tofu), can be used as a bag like a Middle Eastern pitta bread. Here, a generous amount of chopped spring onion and other aromatic ingredients fill the bag. In Japan, spring onions are thought to prevent colds in the winter.

SERVES 4

1 packet thin deep-fried tofu (abura-age)
4 spring onions (scallions), trimmed and
   very finely chopped
about 15ml/1 tbsp shoyu
1 garlic clove, grated or crushed
30ml/2 tbsp lightly toasted
   sesame seeds

COOK'S TIP
If the thin deep-fried tofu prove difficult to open, use a round-bladed knife and insert the blade, moving it gently from side to side, to gradually open out the bag.

1 Put the thin deep-fried tofu in a sieve and pour hot water from a kettle over it to wash off any excess oil. Drain and gently dry on kitchen paper.

2 Put one thin deep-fried tofu on a chopping board and roll over several times with a rolling pin. Cut the thin deep-fried tofu in half and carefully open at the cut part to make two bags. Repeat with the remaining piece.

3 Mix together the spring onions, shoyu, garlic and sesame seeds in a small bowl. Check the seasoning and add more shoyu, if required.

4 Spoon equal quantities of the filling into the four bags. Grill (broil) under a preheated grill (broiler) at high for 3–4 minutes on each side, or until crisp and lightly browned.

5 With a sharp knife, cut each tofu bag into four triangles and arrange them on four small plates. Serve hot.

SU-MESHI in TOFU BAGS

These delightful little tofu pockets are served with soy sauce-based seasonings and filled with su-meshi, sushi rice.

SERVES 4

8 fresh abura-age or 275g/10oz can ready-
    to-use abura-age (contains 16 halves)
900ml/1½ pints/3¾ cups water and
    10ml/2 tsp dashi-no-moto (Japanese
    stock granules)
90ml/6 tbsp caster (superfine) sugar
30ml/2 tbsp sake (Japanese rice wine)
70ml/4½ tbsp shoyu
generous 1 quantity su-meshi (sushi rice),
    made with 40ml/8 tsp sugar
30ml/2 tbsp toasted white sesame seeds
gari, to garnish (see Cook's Tip)

COOK'S TIP
Gari are pale pink ginger pickles available
from Japanese food stores. They have a
pleasantly refreshing flavour.

1 Par-boil the fresh abura-age in rapidly boiling water for about 1 minute. Drain under cold running water and leave to cool. Squeeze the excess water out gently. Cut each sheet in half and carefully pull open the cut end to make bags. If you are using canned abura-age, drain the liquid.

2 Lay the abura-age bags in a large pan. Pour in the dashi stock to cover and bring to the boil. Reduce the heat and cover, then simmer for 20 minutes. Add the sugar in three batches during this time, shaking the pan to dissolve it. Simmer for a further 15 minutes.

3 Add the sake. Shake the pan again, and add the shoyu in three batches. Simmer until almost all the liquid has evaporated. Transfer the abura-age to a wide sieve and leave to drain.

4 Mix the su-meshi and sesame seeds in a wet mixing bowl. Wet your hands, take a little su-meshi and shape it into a rectangular block. Open one abura-age bag and insert the block. Press the edges together to close the bag.

5 Once all the bags have been filled, place them on a large serving plate or individual plates with the bottom of the bag on top. Garnish with a little gari.

DEEP-FRIED TOFU BALLS

There are many variations of these delicious Japanese deep-fried tofu balls called hiryozu,
meaning flying dragon's head. This is one of the easiest to make.

MAKES 16

2 × 300g/11oz packets firm tofu
20g/¾oz carrot, peeled
40g/1½oz green beans
2 large (US extra large) eggs, beaten
30ml/2 tbsp sake (Japanese rice wine)
10ml/2 tsp mirin (sweet rice wine)
5ml/1 tsp salt
10ml/2 tsp shoyu
pinch of caster (superfine) sugar
vegetable oil, for deep-frying

For the lime sauce
45ml/3 tbsp shoyu
juice of ½ lime
5ml/1 tsp rice vinegar

To garnish
300g/11oz mooli (daikon), peeled
2 dried red chillies, halved and seeded
4 chives, finely chopped

1 Drain the tofu and wrap it in a
dishtowel or kitchen paper. Set a
chopping board, or large plate with a
weight, on top and leave for 2 hours, or
until it loses most of its liquid and its
weight is halved.

2 Cut the mooli for the garnish into
about 4cm/1½in thick slices. Make
3–4 holes in each slice with a skewer or
chopstick and insert chilli pieces into the
holes. Leave for 15 minutes, then grate
the mooli and chilli finely.

3 To make the tofu balls, chop the
carrot finely. Trim and cut the beans into
5mm/¼in lengths. Cook both vegetables
for 1 minute in boiling water.

4 In a food processor, process the tofu,
eggs, sake, mirin, salt, shoyu and sugar
until smooth. Transfer to a bowl and mix
in the carrot and beans.

5 Fill a wok or pan with oil 4cm/1½in
deep, and heat to 185°C/365°F.

6 Soak a piece of kitchen paper with a
little vegetable oil, and rub your hands
with it. Scoop 40ml/2½ tbsp of the tofu
mixture in one hand and shape into a
ball by tossing it between your hands.

7 Deep-fry the tofu ball until crisp and
golden brown. Drain on kitchen paper.
Repeat shaping and deep-frying with the
remaining mixture.

8 Arrange the tofu balls on a serving
plate and sprinkle with chives. Put 30ml/
2 tbsp grated mooli in each of four small
bowls. Mix the lime sauce ingredients in
a serving bowl. Serve the balls with the
lime sauce to be mixed with grated
mooli by each guest.

FALAFEL with HUMMUS

Fresh, lightly spiced home-made hummus goes perfectly with these delicious, crunchy tofu balls. Serve with warm pitta bread and a sweet chilli dip.

SERVES 4–6

30ml/2 tbsp vegetable oil
2 large onions, finely chopped
3 garlic cloves, crushed
500g/1¼lb firm tofu, drained
200g/7oz/3¾ cups fresh breadcrumbs
15g/½oz bunch fresh parsley,
    finely chopped
15ml/1 tbsp roasted sesame oil
45ml/3 tbsp soy sauce
50g/2oz/4 tbsp sesame seeds, toasted
5ml/1 tsp ground cumin
15ml/1 tbsp ground turmeric
60ml/4 tbsp tahini (see Cook's Tips)
juice of 1 lemon
1.5ml/¼ tsp cayenne pepper

For the hummus
150g/5oz/¾ cup dried chickpeas
juice of 2 lemons
2 garlic cloves, sliced
30ml/2 tbsp olive oil
pinch of cayenne pepper
150ml/¼ pint/⅔ cup tahini
salt and ground black pepper
extra olive oil and cayenne pepper,
    for sprinkling
flat leaf parsley, to garnish

1 To make the hummus, put the chickpeas in a bowl, pour in plenty of cold water to cover, then leave to soak overnight.

2 Drain the chickpeas and place in a pan. Add fresh cold water to cover, bring to the boil and boil rapidly for 10 minutes. Reduce the heat and simmer gently for about 1–1½ hours, until tender. You may need to cook the chickpeas for longer, depending on how long they have been stored. Drain.

3 Meanwhile make the falafel. Heat the vegetable oil in a large frying pan and sauté the onion and garlic over a medium heat for 2–3 minutes, until softened. Set aside to cool slightly.

4 Preheat the oven to 180°C/350°F/ Gas 4. In a large bowl, mix together the remaining ingredients until well blended, then stir in the onion mixture.

5 Form the mixture into 2.5cm/1in diameter balls and place them on an oiled baking sheet. Bake for 30 minutes, or until crusty on the outside but still moist on the inside.

6 Meanwhile, place the chickpeas in a food processor and process to a smooth purée, pulsing the machine and scraping down the chickpeas once or twice. Add the lemon juice, garlic, olive oil, cayenne pepper and tahini and blend until smooth and creamy, scraping the mixture down from the sides of the bowl.

7 Season the purée with salt and pepper to taste and transfer the hummus to a serving dish. Sprinkle with olive oil and cayenne pepper and garnish with a few parsley sprigs. Serve with the hot falafel, speared with cocktail sticks (toothpicks).

COOK'S TIPS
• For convenience, canned chickpeas can be used instead. Allow two 400g/14oz cans and drain them thoroughly. Rinse well under cold running water and drain again before processing.
• Tahini, a paste made from sesame seeds, can be purchased from most supermarkets or health-food stores. Stir thoroughly before use to incorporate the oil that rises to the surface of the jar on standing.
• If you like, process the tofu in a blender or food processor to a smooth paste before mixing with the other ingredients.

GRILLED VEGETABLE STICKS

For this tasty kebab-style dish, made with tofu, konnyaku – the processed corm of the konjac plant – and aubergine, you will need 40 bamboo skewers, soaked in water overnight.

SERVES 4

300g/11oz firm tofu
250g/9oz packet konnyaku
2 small aubergines (eggplant)
25ml/1½ tbsp toasted sesame oil

For the yellow and green sauces
45ml/3 tbsp shiro-miso
15ml/1 tbsp caster (superfine) sugar
5 young spinach leaves
2.5ml/½ tsp sansho
salt

For the red sauce
15ml/1 tbsp aka-miso
5ml/1 tsp caster (superfine) sugar
5ml/1 tsp mirin

To garnish
pinch of white poppy seeds
15ml/1 tbsp toasted sesame seeds

1 Drain the liquid from the tofu packet and wrap the tofu in three layers of kitchen paper. Set a chopping board on top to press out the remaining liquid. Leave for 30 minutes, until the excess liquid has been absorbed by the kitchen paper. Cut into eight 7.5 × 2 × 1cm/ 3 × ¾ × ½in slices.

2 Drain the liquid from the konnyaku. Cut it in half and put in a small pan with enough water to cover. Bring to the boil and cook for about 5 minutes. Drain well and cut it into eight 6 × 2 × 1cm/ 2½ × ¾ × ½in slices.

3 Cut the aubergines in half lengthways, then halve the thickness to make four flat slices. Place in a dish, add cold water to cover and leave to soak for 15 minutes. Drain well and pat thoroughly dry on kitchen paper.

4 To make the yellow sauce, mix the shiro-miso and sugar in a pan, then cook over a low heat, stirring to dissolve the sugar. Remove from the heat. Place half the sauce in a small bowl.

5 Blanch the spinach leaves in rapidly boiling water with a pinch of salt for 30 seconds and drain, then cool under cold running water. Squeeze out the water and chop finely.

6 Transfer to a mortar and pound to a paste using a pestle. Mix the paste and sansho pepper into the bowl of yellow sauce to make the green sauce.

7 Put all the red sauce ingredients in a small pan and cook over a low heat, stirring constantly, until the sugar has dissolved. Remove from the heat.

8 Pierce the slices of tofu, konnyaku and aubergine with two bamboo skewers each. Heat the grill (broiler) to high. Brush the aubergine slices with sesame oil and grill (broil) for 7–8 minutes on each side. Turn several times.

9 Grill the konnyaku and tofu slices for 3–5 minutes each side, or until lightly browned. Remove them from the heat.

10 Spread the red miso sauce on the aubergine slices. Spread one side of the tofu slices with green sauce and one side of the konnyaku with the yellow miso sauce. Grill the slices for 1–2 minutes. Sprinkle the aubergines with poppy seeds. Sprinkle the konnyaku with sesame seeds and serve all together.

THAI TEMPEH CAKES with DIPPING SAUCE

Here, nutty-tasting tempeh is combined with a fragrant blend of lemon grass, fresh coriander and ginger and formed into small patties before being fried.

MAKES 8

1 lemon grass stalk, outer leaves removed
    and inside chopped
2 garlic cloves, chopped
2 spring onions (scallions), chopped
2 shallots, chopped
2 chillies, seeded and chopped
2.5cm/1in piece fresh root ginger,
    chopped
60ml/4 tbsp chopped fresh coriander
    (cilantro), plus extra to garnish
250g/9oz tempeh, thawed if frozen,
    sliced
15ml/1 tbsp lime juice
5ml/1 tsp sugar
45ml/3 tbsp plain (all-purpose) flour
1 large (US extra large) egg, lightly beaten
vegetable oil, for frying
salt and ground black pepper

For the dipping sauce
45ml/3 tbsp mirin (see Cook's Tip)
45ml/3 tbsp white wine vinegar
2 spring onions (scallions), thinly sliced
15ml/1 tbsp sugar
2 chillies, finely chopped
30ml/2 tbsp chopped fresh
    coriander (cilantro)
large pinch of salt

1 To make the dipping sauce, mix together the mirin, vinegar, spring onions, sugar, chillies, coriander and salt in a small bowl and set aside.

2 Place the lemon grass, garlic, spring onions, shallots, chillies, ginger and coriander in a food processor or blender and process to a coarse paste. Add the tempeh, lime juice and sugar, then process to combine. Add the seasoning, flour and egg. Process again until the mixture forms a coarse, sticky paste.

COOK'S TIP
Mirin is a sweet sake, or rice wine, with a delicate flavour. It is designed to be used for cooking and is relatively inexpensive. It is available from Japanese food stores and some large supermarkets.

3 Take one-eighth of the tempeh mixture at a time and form into balls with your hands – the mixture will be quite sticky, so it may help to dampen your palms. Gently flatten the balls.

4 Heat enough oil to cover the base of a large frying pan. Fry the tempeh cakes for 5–6 minutes, turning once, until golden. Drain on kitchen paper. Garnish and serve warm with the dipping sauce.

SILKEN TOFU and AVOCADO DIPPING SAUCE

*This rich and creamy dip is not unlike guacamole and can be served with tortilla chips
or a selection of fresh and crunchy vegetables.*

SERVES 4

1 large ripe avocado
10 fresh chives
juice of 1 lime
25g/1oz/1 cup chopped fresh
    coriander (cilantro)
15ml/1 tbsp finely chopped spring
    onion (scallion)
45ml/3 tbsp silken tofu
salt and freshly ground black pepper
shreds of spring onions (scallions),
    to garnish

COOK'S TIP
Make sure that the dipping sauce is tightly
covered with clear film (plastic wrap)
before chilling in the refrigerator, as
avocado discolours, turning an
unattractive shade of greyish brown if
it is exposed to air for long.

1 Place the avocado in a pan of boiling
water and turn constantly for 1 minute.
Remove from the pan and peel off the
skin – it should come off easily. Cut the
avocado in half and remove the stone
(pit) with the point of the knife.

2 Mash the avocado in a bowl with a
fork until the flesh is completely smooth,
then snip in the fresh chives.

3 Stir in the lime juice, coriander and
spring onion and mix well, then fold in
the silken tofu and season to taste with
salt and pepper. Cover and chill for
about 1 hour before serving, garnished
with spring onion shreds.

VARIATION
For a spicier dipping sauce, stir in a
seeded and finely chopped chilli in step 3.

VEGETABLE SALAD with TAHINI TOFU DIP

*This is an ideal appetizer for those who want to follow a healthy-eating regime – raw
vegetables and an almost fat-free dressing. The secret to a superb salad is to buy the
freshest vegetables possible – or even better, grow your own.*

SERVES 4

500g/1¼lb mixed young raw vegetables,
    such as fennel, vine or cherry
    tomatoes, carrots, chicory (Belgian
    endive), cauliflower florets and
    red, yellow or orange (bell)
    peppers, prepared

For the dressing
1 garlic clove
50ml/2fl oz/¼ cup tahini
115g/4oz silken tofu
30ml/2 tbsp lemon juice
50ml/2fl oz/¼ cup sunflower oil
1 spring onion (scallion), finely chopped
15ml/1 tbsp light soy sauce
about 50ml/2fl oz/¼ cup water
2.5ml/½ tsp finely ground salt

1 Arrange all the vegetables in groups
according to type on a tray or platter,
leaving room for the bowl of dressing.

2 Crush the garlic with the flat side of a
knife blade, place in a small bowl and stir
in the tahini. Stir in the tofu and lemon
juice and then slowly drizzle in the oil.

3 Add the spring onion, reserving a few
of the green leaves as a garnish. Stir in
the soy sauce with enough water to
make a smooth, thick creamy dressing.
Season to taste with salt and spoon into
a serving bowl. Garnish with the
reserved spring onion and serve with
the prepared vegetables.

SALADS AND SIDE DISHES

Silken tofu is an invaluable ingredient for making creamy textured dressings and sauces, whether in a rich-tasting egg-free mayonnaise combined with crunchy coleslaw or a creamy garlic dip to serve with potato wedges. Firm tofu provides a pleasing contrast in texture and appearance when mixed with salad leaves, lightly cooked vegetables and, classically, noodles and rice.

BROCCOLI and MUSHROOM SALAD with TOFU

This bold-flavoured salad combines satisfyingly contrasting textures in the tofu and vegetables. It could be served with buckwheat and a pinch of dried chilli flakes to make a delicious meal.

SERVES 4

250g/9oz firm tofu, drained and cubed,
    or 250g/9oz smoked tofu, cubed
250g/9oz broccoli, cut into large florets
15ml/1 tbsp olive oil
1 garlic clove, finely chopped
350g/12oz chestnut mushrooms, sliced
4 spring onions (scallions), thinly sliced
75g/3oz/¾ cup pine nuts, toasted

For the marinade
1 garlic clove, crushed
2.5cm/1in piece fresh root ginger,
    finely grated
45ml/3 tbsp soy sauce
45ml/3 tbsp tamari soy sauce
45ml/3 tbsp Chinese rice wine or
    dry sherry
1.5ml/¼ tsp cumin seeds, toasted and
    coarsely crushed
1.5ml/¼ tsp caster (superfine) sugar
ground black pepper

1 Prepare the marinade by stirring all the ingredients together in a jug (pitcher). Place the tofu cubes in a bowl, pour in the marinade, toss to coat and leave to marinate for at least 1 hour.

2 Meanwhile steam the broccoli for 4–5 minutes, until just tender then refresh under cold running water. Drain well then place in a large bowl.

3 Heat the oil in a large, heavy frying pan or wok. Add the garlic and stir-fry over a low heat for 1 minute, until golden. Do not allow the garlic to burn.

4 Add the mushrooms and fry over a high heat for 4–5 minutes, until cooked through. Add to the broccoli and season with ground black pepper.

5 Once marinated, toss the tofu and its marinade with the broccoli, mushrooms and spring onions. Sprinkle with the pine nuts and serve immediately.

CHICORY and AVOCADO SALAD with RICH TOFU-DILL DRESSING

In this fresh, crunchy salad the bitterness of the chicory is perfectly complemented by the rocket, crunchy walnuts and smooth avocado.

SERVES 4

3 chicory (Belgian endive) heads, leaves
    separated, washed and dried
50g/2oz rocket (arugula), washed
    and dried
2 large ripe avocados
juice of ½ lemon
90g/3½oz/scant 1 cup walnut halves
sea salt and ground black pepper

For the dressing
15g/½oz/½ cup dill, any tough
    stalks removed
1 small garlic clove, crushed
juice of 1 lemon
5ml/1 tsp clear honey
5ml/1 tsp soy sauce
350g/12oz silken tofu
5ml/1 tsp French mustard
pinch of salt
50ml/2fl oz/¼ cup olive oil

2 Divide the avocado slices evenly among the plates, arranging them among the chicory and rocket leaves.

3 Sprinkle over the walnuts and season lightly with salt and pepper.

4 Make the dressing by blending all the ingredients except the oil in a food processor or blender. With the machine running, gradually add the oil. Taste and adjust the seasoning. Drizzle the dressing over the salad and serve immediately.

1 Toss the chicory and rocket leaves together in a bowl and then heap on to four individual serving plates. Peel, stone (pit) and slice the avocados, then toss in the lemon juice to prevent the slices from going brown.

VARIATION
The dressing could be made with other fresh herbs, such as coriander (cilantro), basil or parsley.

COOK'S TIP
Keep any remaining dressing in the refrigerator for use on another salad, as it is very versatile.

CRUNCHY COLESLAW with TOFU MAYONNAISE

*The creamy, crunchy freshness of this coleslaw makes it the ideal accompaniment to
vegetable burgers or chargrilled vegetables at a summer barbecue. Silken tofu makes
a wonderfully rich and creamy mayonnaise – and it's good for you.*

SERVES 4–6

200g/7oz white cabbage, shredded
200g/7oz red cabbage, shredded
130g/4½oz carrots, coarsely grated
1 onion, thinly sliced
sea salt and ground black pepper

For the tofu mayonnaise
175g/6oz silken tofu, drained
juice of ½ lemon
2.5ml/½ tsp Dijon mustard
dash of Tabasco sauce
105ml/7 tbsp olive oil

VARIATION
Fresh herbs, such as basil, dill or
coriander (cilantro) or mint, or a mixture
of herbs can be added to the mayonnaise.
Simply process with the other ingredients
before adding the oil.

1 First make the tofu mayonnaise by
placing all the ingredients except the
olive oil in a blender or food processor
and processing until smooth and
thoroughly combined.

COOK'S TIP
Cover the mayonnaise tightly and store in
the refrigerator, where it will stay fresh
for up to 1 week.

2 Season to taste and then with the
machine running, add the oil in a slow
and steady stream until the mixture
thickens. Cover and chill or use
immediately on the coleslaw.

3 To make the coleslaw, combine the
white and red cabbage, carrots and
onion in a bowl then add the
mayonnaise and toss together well.

GREEN BEAN and CHERRY TOMATO SALAD with TOFU PESTO

*This classic salad of green beans and sweet cherry tomatoes is combined with a non-dairy
version of pesto that is creamy and delicious. The pesto will also work well on pasta, and
can be stored in an airtight container for later use.*

SERVES 4

600g/1lb 6oz green beans, trimmed
30ml/2 tbsp olive oil
4 shallots, finely chopped
400g/14oz cherry tomatoes, halved

For the tofu pesto
1 tomato, chopped
2 garlic cloves, coarsely chopped
30g/1¼oz fresh basil or
　½ bunch of fresh parsley, any
　tough stems removed and the
　rest chopped
105ml/7 tbsp olive oil
150g/5oz silken tofu
dash of lemon juice
50g/2oz/½ cup ground almonds
sea salt and ground black pepper

1 First make the pesto by processing the
tomato and garlic in a blender or food
processor until smooth. Add the rest of
ingredients, season and blend again until
the sauce is smooth and creamy.

2 Blanch the beans in boiling salted water
for 2 minutes, or until just tender. Drain.

3 Meanwhile, heat the oil in a frying pan
over a gentle heat and stir-fry the
shallots for 4 minutes until softened.

4 Add the blanched beans and cherry
tomatoes to the pan with the pesto.
Toss together to mix well and serve hot
or leave to cool, then chill to serve cold.

FRIED TOFU and RICE NOODLE SALAD

A light and refreshing salad, this is a meal in itself. With a pack of marinated tofu, a bunch of spring onions and some fresh coriander picked up on the way home from work, it is also a very quick and easy supper made from store-cupboard ingredients.

SERVES 4

200g/7oz cellophane noodles
8 spring onions (scallions), thinly sliced
300g/11oz marinated deep-fried tofu
about 2.5ml/½ tsp dried chilli flakes
grated rind and juice of 1 lemon
5cm/2in piece fresh root ginger, sliced into
    fine batons (optional)
1 bunch fresh coriander (cilantro) or
    parsley, chopped
about 30ml/2 tbsp soy sauce
30ml/2 tbsp toasted sesame oil
65g/2½oz/½ cup sesame or sunflower
    seeds, toasted, or 75 g/3 oz/
    ¾ cup peanuts

1 Cover the noodles with boiling water, leave for 5–10 minutes, or according to the manufacturer's instructions, then drain and rinse under cold running water. Place in a large bowl.

2 Add the spring onions, tofu, chilli flakes, lemon rind and juice, ginger, if using, coriander, soy sauce, sesame oil and seeds or nuts and toss together. Check the seasoning and serve.

TOFU and WILD RICE SALAD

The flavours in this salad are influenced by the cuisines of North Africa and the eastern seaboards of the Mediterranean. It goes particularly well with chargrilled vegetables such as red onions, tomatoes, courgettes and peppers.

SERVES 4

175g/6oz/scant 1 cup basmati rice
50g/2oz/generous ¼ cup wild rice
250g/9oz firm tofu, drained and cubed
25g/1oz preserved lemon, finely chopped
  (see Cook's Tip)
20g/¾oz bunch of fresh
  parsley, chopped

For the dressing
1 garlic clove, crushed
10ml/2 tsp clear honey
10ml/2 tsp of the preserved lemon juice
15ml/1 tbsp balsamic vinegar
15ml/1 tbsp olive oil
1 small fresh red chilli, seeded and
  finely chopped
5ml/1 tsp harissa paste (optional)
sea salt and ground black pepper

1 Cook the basmati rice and the wild rice in separate pans until tender. The basmati will take about 10–15 minutes to cook while the wild rice will take about 45–50 minutes. Drain, rinse under cold water and drain again, then place in a large bowl together.

2 Meanwhile whisk together all the dressing ingredients in a small bowl. Add the tofu, stir to coat and leave to marinate while the rice cooks.

VARIATIONS
Keep an eye open for rose harissa paste, which is available from the special range in some large supermarkets or from delicatessens or food halls. It is exceptionally delicious in this recipe and still fiery hot.

3 Gently fold the tofu, marinade, preserved lemon and parsley into the rice, check the seasoning and serve.

COOK'S TIP
Preserved lemons, packed in salt, are available from Middle Eastern delicatessens or from large food halls and some supermarkets.

STIR-FRIED CRISPY TOFU

Asparagus is not only elegant but also delicious. This fabulous Thai dish, combining tofu and asparagus, is the perfect side dish to serve at a dinner party.

SERVES 2

250g/9oz deep-fried tofu cubes
30ml/2 tbsp groundnut (peanut) oil
15ml/1 tbsp Thai green curry paste
30ml/2 tbsp light soy sauce
2 kaffir lime leaves, rolled into cylinders
    and thinly sliced
30ml/2 tbsp granulated sugar
150ml/¼ pint/⅔ cup vegetable stock
250g/9oz Asian asparagus, trimmed and
    sliced into 5cm/2in lengths
30ml/2 tbsp roasted peanuts,
    finely chopped

VARIATION

Substitute slim carrot batons, baby leeks or small broccoli florets for the Asian asparagus, if you like.

1 Preheat the grill (broiler) to medium. Place the tofu cubes in a grill pan and grill (broil) for 2–3 minutes, then turn them over and continue to cook until they are crisp and golden brown all over. Watch them carefully; they must not be allowed to burn.

2 Heat the oil in a wok or heavy frying pan. Add the green curry paste and cook over a medium heat, stirring constantly, for 1–2 minutes, until it gives off its aroma.

3 Stir the soy sauce, lime leaves, sugar and vegetable stock into the wok or pan and mix well. Bring to the boil, then reduce the heat to low so that the mixture is just simmering.

4 Add the asparagus and simmer gently for 5 minutes. Meanwhile, chop each piece of tofu into four, then add to the pan with the peanuts.

5 Toss to coat all the ingredients in the sauce, then spoon into a warmed dish and serve immediately.

ROASTED PEPPERS with TOFU and PINE NUTS

Here is an alternative to the more usual meat- or rice-stuffed peppers. The use of garlic or herb olive oil enhances the flavour.

SERVES 4

4 red (bell) peppers
1 orange (bell) pepper, seeded and
   coarsely chopped
1 yellow (bell) pepper, seeded and
   coarsely chopped
60ml/4 tbsp garlic or herb olive oil
250g/9oz firm tofu
50g/2oz/½ cup pine nuts

1 Preheat the oven to 220°C/425°F/ Gas 7. Cut the red peppers in half, leaving the stalks intact, and discard the seeds. Place the red pepper halves on a baking sheet and fill with the chopped orange and yellow peppers. Drizzle with half the garlic or herb olive oil and bake for 25 minutes, until the edges of the peppers are beginning to char.

2 Meanwhile, unpack the tofu blocks and discard the liquid, then wrap the tofu in layers of kitchen paper. Put a large plate on top as a weight and leave for 30 minutes to allow the excess liquid to be absorbed by the paper.

3 Cut the tofu into cubes using a sharp knife.

4 Remove the peppers from the oven, but leave the oven switched on. Tuck the tofu cubes in among the chopped orange and yellow peppers. Sprinkle evenly with the pine nuts and drizzle with the remaining garlic or herb oil. Bake for a further 15 minutes, or until well browned. Serve warm or at room temperature.

PAN-FRIED TOFU with CARAMELIZED SAUCE

This satisfying dish is a modern take on the vegetarian cuisine developed by Buddhist monks in Japan. If you don't have mirin, use Amontillado sherry instead.

SERVES 4

2 × 300g/11oz packets firm tofu
4 garlic cloves
10ml/2 tsp vegetable oil
50g/2oz/¼ cup butter, cut into
    5 equal pieces
watercress, to garnish

For the marinade
4 spring onions (scallions)
60ml/4 tbsp sake (Japanese rice wine)
60ml/4 tbsp shoyu (tamari or sashimi soy
    sauce, if available)
60ml/4 tbsp mirin (sweet rice wine)

1 Unpack the tofu blocks and discard the liquid, then wrap in three layers of kitchen paper. Put a large plate or wooden chopping board on top as a weight and leave for 30 minutes to allow the excess liquid to be absorbed by the paper. This process makes the tofu firmer and, when cooked, it will crisp on the outside.

2 To make the marinade, chop the spring onions finely. Mix with the other marinade ingredients in a ceramic or aluminium tray with sides or a wide, shallow bowl. Leave for 15 minutes.

3 Slice the garlic very thinly to make garlic chips. Heat the vegetable oil in a frying pan or wok and cook the garlic for a few moments until golden. Turn the garlic chips frequently to prevent them from sticking and burning. Scoop them out on to kitchen paper to drain. Reserve the oil in the pan.

4 Unwrap the tofu. Slice one block horizontally in half, then cut each half into four pieces. Repeat with the other tofu block. Soak in the marinade for about 15 minutes.

5 Take out the tofu and wipe off the excess marinade with kitchen paper. Reserve the marinade.

6 Reheat the oil in the frying pan and add one piece of butter. When the oil starts sizzling, reduce the heat to medium and add the pieces of tofu one by one. Cook in one layer, if possible.

7 Cover the pan and cook for about 5–8 minutes on each side, until the edge of the tofu is browned and quite firm. (If the edges burn but the centre is pale, reduce the heat.)

8 Pour the marinade into the pan. Cook for 2 minutes, or until the spring onion is very soft. Remove the tofu with a slotted spoon and arrange four pieces on each of four serving plates. Pour the thickened marinade and spring onion mixture over the tofu and top with a piece of butter. Sprinkle with the garlic chips and garnish with watercress sprigs. Serve immediately while still hot.

COOK'S TIP

If you suffer from gluten intolerance, use tamari soy sauce, which has a rich, robust flavour and is made without wheat. It is available from Asian supermarkets.

TWICE-COOKED TEMPEH

This dish is first pan-fried and then oven-baked in a deeply flavoured sauce.
Serve the tempeh with crispy mixed salad leaves and sliced tomatoes stuffed
into warmed pitta breads.

SERVES 4

45ml/3 tbsp vegetable oil
2 onions, finely chopped
2 garlic cloves, crushed
5ml/1 tsp fennel seeds, crushed
2.5ml/½ tsp chilli flakes
5ml/1 tsp coriander seeds, crushed
5ml/1 tsp cumin seeds, crushed
1 red (bell) pepper, seeded and
    finely chopped
450g/1lb tempeh
115g/4oz Cheddar cheese, grated

For the sauce
30ml/2 tbsp tamari soy sauce
juice of ½ lemon
45ml/3 tbsp molasses or dark brown sugar
30ml/2 tbsp cider (apple cider) vinegar
15ml/1 tbsp English (hot) mustard
90ml/6 tbsp tomato purée (paste)
150ml/¼ pint/⅔ cup water
2–3 dashes Tabasco or other hot pepper
    sauce (optional)
30ml/2 tbsp coarsely chopped flat
    leaf parsley

1 Preheat the oven to 200°C/400°F/
Gas 6. Heat 30ml/2 tbsp of the oil in a
large frying pan or wok and sauté the
onions, garlic and spices for 6–7 minutes,
until golden and softened.

2 Add the pepper and cook for a
further 1–2 minutes, until softened.

3 Whisk together all the sauce
ingredients and add to the pan. Simmer
gently for 2–3 minutes to warm through.
Finally, stir in the parsley.

4 Heat the remaining oil in a large frying
pan and fry the tempeh for 2–3 minutes
on each side, until golden and warmed
through. Transfer to a large, shallow,
heatproof serving dish.

5 Pour the finished sauce over the
tempeh and sprinkle evenly with the
grated cheese. Bake in the oven for
about 10 minutes, until the cheese has
melted and is bubbling.

BRAISED TOFU with MUSHROOMS

Four different kinds of mushrooms combine beautifully with tofu in this recipe. Chinese flavourings enhance all the ingredients to make this the perfect vegetarian side dish to serve at a dinner party.

SERVES 4

350g/12oz firm tofu
2.5ml/½ tsp sesame oil
10ml/2 tsp light soy sauce
15ml/1 tbsp vegetable oil
2 garlic cloves, finely chopped
2.5ml/½ tsp grated fresh root ginger
115g/4oz/scant 2 cups fresh shiitake
    mushrooms, stalks removed
175g/6oz/scant 2 cups fresh
    oyster mushrooms
115g/4oz/scant 2 cups drained, canned
    straw mushrooms
115g/4oz/scant 2 cups button (white)
    mushrooms, halved
15ml/1 tbsp Chinese rice wine or
    dry sherry
15ml/1 tbsp dark soy sauce
90ml/6 tbsp vegetable stock
5ml/1 tsp cornflour (cornstarch)
15ml/1 tbsp cold water
salt and ground white pepper
2 shredded spring onions (scallions),
    to garnish

VARIATION

For a Thai flavour, substitute 5ml/1 tsp Thai fish sauce for the same quantity of soy sauce and use galangal instead of root ginger. Stir-fry 1–2 seeded and chopped fresh red chillies with the garlic and garnish with chopped coriander (cilantro).

1 Put the tofu in a dish or bowl and sprinkle with the sesame oil, light soy sauce and a large pinch of pepper. Leave to marinate for 10 minutes, then drain and cut into 2.5 x 1cm/1 x ½in pieces using a sharp knife.

2 Heat the vegetable oil in a large non-stick frying pan or wok. When the oil is very hot, add the garlic and ginger and stir-fry for a few seconds. Add all the mushrooms and stir-fry for a further 2 minutes.

3 Stir in the Chinese rice wine or dry sherry, dark soy sauce and stock. Season to taste with salt, if necessary, and ground white pepper. Lower the heat and simmer gently for 4 minutes.

4 Place the cornflour in a bowl with the water. Mix to make a smooth paste. Stir the cornflour mixture into the pan or wok and cook, stirring constantly to prevent lumps, until thickened.

5 Carefully add the pieces of tofu, toss gently to coat thoroughly in the sauce and simmer for 2 minutes.

6 Sprinkle the shredded spring onions over the top of the mixture to garnish, transfer to a warm serving dish or individual plates and serve immediately.

COOK'S TIPS

• If fresh shiitake mushrooms are not available, use dried Chinese mushrooms. Soak them in hot water for about 20–30 minutes, then drain. Use the soaking liquid instead of vegetable stock for a more intense flavour.
• Straw mushrooms, so called because they are grown on beds of straw, are rarely available fresh in the West. However, they are widely available canned. Their main contribution to this dish – and to Chinese cooking in general – is their slippery texture rather than their flavour which is quite bland.
• Chinese rice wine has a rich, mellow flavour and is available from Asian food stores and many supermarkets. It is not the same as Japanese mirin; dry sherry is a better substitute.

HOT POTATO WEDGES with GARLIC TOFU DIP

Tofu makes a fabulous dip that is cool and creamy – the perfect foil for crispy hot potato wedges.

SERVES 4

6 potatoes, scrubbed
15ml/1 tbsp cumin seeds, ground
2.5–5ml/½–1 tsp cayenne pepper
grated rind of 2 limes or 1 lemon
45ml/3 tbsp olive oil
sea salt and ground black pepper

For the garlic tofu dip
1 garlic clove, crushed
175g/6oz silken tofu
dash of lemon juice
25ml/1½ tbsp olive oil
10g/¼oz fresh mint, stalks
   removed (optional)

COOK'S TIPS
• Garlic tofu dip is good with any roasted root vegetables, such as carrots, swede (rutabaga), celeriac and parsnips.
• If covered, the dip will keep in the refrigerator for up to 1 week.

1 Cut the potatoes lengthways in half, then cut each half lengthways into thirds or quarters to make wedges. Place them in a shallow dish and sprinkle over the spices, citrus rind, oil and seasoning. Toss together and leave to marinate for at least 30 minutes. Meanwhile, preheat the oven to 220°C/425°F/Gas 7.

2 Place the potato wedges in a roasting pan and bake for 30–35 minutes, until golden and tender, turning occasionally.

3 Meanwhile, make the garlic tofu dip by placing all the ingredients, except the oil, in a blender or food processor and processing until smooth.

4 With the machine running, gradually add the olive oil in a slow, steady stream until the dip is smooth and thickened. Season with salt and pepper to taste, then pour into a serving bowl. Transfer the potato wedges to a warm serving dish and serve with the dip.

COURGETTES and TOFU with TOMATO SAUCE

*This Mediterranean-style dish is great hot or cold, and improves given a day or two
covered in the refrigerator. It makes the perfect accompaniment to a nut or meat roast.*

SERVES 4

30ml/2 tbsp olive oil
2 garlic cloves, finely chopped
4 large courgettes (zucchini), thinly sliced
   on the diagonal
250g/9oz firm tofu, drained and cubed
1 lemon
sea salt and ground black pepper

For the tomato sauce
10ml/2 tsp balsamic vinegar
5ml/1 tsp sugar
300ml/½ pint/1¼ cups passata (bottled
   strained tomatoes)
small bunch of fresh mint or
   parsley, chopped

1 First, make the tomato sauce, Place all
the ingredients in a small pan and heat
through gently, stirring occasionally.

2 Meanwhile, heat the olive oil in a large
non-stick wok or frying pan until very
hot, then add the garlic and stir-fry for
30 seconds, until golden. Add the
courgettes and stir-fry over a high heat
for about 5–6 minutes, or until golden
around the edges. Remove from the pan.

VARIATIONS
• The courgette slices could also be
grilled (broiled) or cooked on the
barbecue, instead of being fried, and then
added to the fried garlic before the tofu
cubes are browned.
• Aubergine (eggplant) slices could be
used instead of the courgettes, but more
olive oil may be needed to fry them
initially, as they have a tendency to soak
up oil like a sponge.

3 Add the tofu to the pan and brown
for a few minutes. Turn gently, then
brown again. Grate the rind from half
the lemon and reserve for the garnish.
Squeeze the lemon juice over the tofu.

4 Season to taste with sea salt and
pepper, then leave to sizzle until all the
lemon juice has evaporated. Gently stir
the courgettes into the tofu until well
combined, then remove the wok or pan
from the heat.

5 Transfer the courgettes and tofu to a
warm serving dish and pour the tomato
sauce over the top. Sprinkle with the
grated lemon rind, Taste and season with
more salt and pepper, if necessary, and
serve immediately.

VEGETARIAN MAIN MEALS

The imaginative, mouthwatering recipes in this chapter demonstrate how indispensable tofu is in the vegetarian kitchen. It plays a starring role in burgers, wraps, kebabs and stir-fries, and in rice and pasta dishes too. Influences from around the world are incorporated into these recipes – from Mexican Tortillas to Teriyaki Soba Noodles and from Vegetable Moussaka to Indian Mee Goreng.

PEANUT and TOFU CUTLETS

These delicious patties make a filling and satisfying midweek meal served with lightly steamed green vegetables or a crisp salad, and a tangy salsa or ketchup.

SERVES 4

90g/3½oz/½ cup brown rice
15ml/1 tbsp vegetable oil
1 onion, finely chopped
1 garlic clove, crushed
200g/7oz/1¾ cups peanuts
small bunch of fresh coriander (cilantro)
    or parsley, chopped (optional)
250g/9oz firm tofu, drained and crumbled
30ml/2 tbsp soy sauce
30ml/2 tbsp olive oil, for shallow frying

VARIATIONS
The herbs and nuts can be varied. Try the following combinations:
• Walnuts with rosemary or sage
• Cashew nuts with coriander (cilantro) or parsley
• Hazelnuts with parsley, thyme or sage.

1 Cook the rice according to the instructions on the packet until tender, then drain. Heat the vegetable oil in a large, heavy frying pan and cook the onion and garlic over a low heat, stirring occasionally, for about 5 minutes, until softened and golden.

2 Meanwhile, spread out the peanuts on a baking sheet and toast under the grill (broiler) for a few minutes, until browned. Place the peanuts, onion, garlic, rice, tofu, coriander or parsley, if using, and soy sauce in a blender or food processor and process until the mixture comes together in a thick paste.

3 Divide the paste into eight equal-size mounds and form each mound into a cutlet shape or square.

4 Heat the olive oil for shallow frying in a large, heavy frying pan. Add the cutlets, in two batches if necessary, and cook for 5–10 minutes on each side, until golden and heated through. Remove from the pan with a fish slice or metal spatula and drain on kitchen paper. Keep warm while you cook the remaining batch, then serve immediately.

VEGETABLE TOFU BURGERS

These soft golden patties are stuffed full of delicious vegetables. They are quick and easy to make and very popular with kids. Serve in sesame seed baps with salad and ketchup.

SERVES 4

4 potatoes, peeled and cubed
250g/9oz frozen mixed vegetables, such
    as corn, green beans, (bell) peppers
45ml/3 tbsp vegetable oil
2 leeks, coarsely chopped
1 garlic clove, crushed
250g/9oz firm tofu, drained and crumbled
30ml/2 tbsp soy sauce
15ml/1 tbsp tomato purée (paste)
115g/4oz/2 cups fresh breadcrumbs
small bunch of fresh coriander (cilantro)
    or parsley (optional)
sea salt and ground black pepper

COOK'S TIP
To preserve their vitamins, cook the
potatoes whole for 20 minutes, then peel.

1 Cook the potatoes in salted, boiling water for 10–12 minutes, until tender, then drain. Meanwhile, cook the frozen vegetables in a separate pan of salted, boiling water for 5 minutes, or until tender, then drain well.

2 Meanwhile, heat 15ml/1 tbsp of the oil in a large frying pan. Add the leeks and garlic and cook over a low heat, stirring occasionally, for about 5 minutes, until softened and golden.

3 Mash the potatoes, then add the vegetables and all the other ingredients except the oil but including the cooked leeks and garlic. Season to taste, then mix together well and divide into eight equal-size mounds.

4 Shape each mound into a burger. Heat another 15ml/1 tbsp oil in the frying pan. Cook four burgers at a time over a gentle heat for 4–5 minutes on each side, until golden brown and warmed through. Repeat with the remaining four burgers, using the remaining oil. Keep the first batch warm in a low oven.

MEXICAN TOFU TORTILLAS

A succulent, lightly spiced mixture of tofu, vegetables and kidney beans is served in tortilla wraps with grated cheese and freshly made guacamole. This is a great idea for a mid-week family supper or an informal dinner party.

SERVES 4

30ml/2 tbsp olive oil
1 red (bell) pepper, seeded and
    finely diced
1 garlic clove, finely chopped
1 small red onion, finely chopped
250g/9oz firm tofu, drained
400g/14oz can red kidney beans, drained
    and rinsed
juice of ½ lemon
15ml/1 tbsp chilli sauce or 2.5ml/½ tsp
    dried chilli flakes (optional)
15ml/1 tbsp soy sauce
small bunch of fresh coriander (cilantro),
    chopped (optional)
8 × 18cm/7in flour tortillas
sea salt and ground black pepper
50g/2oz mature (sharp) Cheddar cheese or
    soya cheese, grated (optional) to serve

For the guacamole
2 ripe avocados
50g/2oz cherry tomatoes, peeled
    and chopped
½ shallot, finely chopped
juice of ½ lemon

1 Heat the oil in a large frying pan. Add the red pepper, onion and garlic and cook over a medium heat, stirring occasionally, for about 5 minutes, until softened and golden.

2 Add the tofu, kidney beans, lemon juice, chilli sauce, soy sauce and coriander and season with sea salt and pepper to taste, then heat through gently, breaking up the tofu with the back of a wooden spoon.

3 Warm the tortillas individually in a heavy frying pan or stacked in the microwave, according to the manufacturer's instructions, then spoon the filling in a line down the centre of each and roll up. Place on a serving platter or individual plates.

4 To make the guacamole, peel the avocados, remove the stones (pits) and chop the flesh. Process in a blender or food processor with the cherry tomatoes, shallot, lemon juice and seasoning. Alternatively, place in a bowl and mash with a fork.

TOFU and PEPPER KEBABS

A simple coating of ground, dry-roasted peanuts pressed on to cubed tofu provides plenty of additional texture and colour along with the red and green peppers. These tasty and easy-to-make kebabs can also be cooked on a barbecue, if you like.

SERVES 2

250g/9oz firm tofu
50g/2oz/½ cup dry-roasted peanuts
2 red (bell) peppers
2 green (bell) peppers
60ml/4 tbsp sweet chilli dipping sauce

1 Pat the tofu dry on kitchen paper and then cut it into small cubes. Grind the peanuts in a blender or food processor and transfer to a plate. Turn the tofu cubes in the ground nuts to coat.

COOK'S TIP
Chilli sauces vary from fairly mild to searingly hot, while some are quite sweet.

2 Preheat the grill (broiler) to medium. Halve and seed the peppers, and cut them into large chunks. Thread the chunks of pepper on to four large skewers with the tofu cubes and place on a foil-lined grill rack.

3 Grill (broil) the kebabs, turning frequently, for 10–12 minutes, or until the peppers and peanuts are beginning to brown. Transfer the kebabs to warmed plates and serve immediately with the dipping sauce.

SWEET-and-SOUR VEGETABLES with TOFU

Big, bold and beautiful, this is a hearty stir-fry that will satisfy the hungriest guests.
Stir-fries are always a good choice when entertaining as they take a short time to cook.

SERVES 4

4 shallots
3 garlic cloves
30ml/2 tbsp groundnut
    (peanut) oil
250g/9oz Chinese leaves (Chinese
    cabbage), shredded
8 baby corn cobs,
    sliced diagonally
2 red (bell) peppers, seeded and
    thinly sliced
200g/7oz/1¾ cups mangetouts (snow
    peas), trimmed and sliced
250g/9oz firm tofu, rinsed, drained and
    cut in 1cm/½in cubes
60ml/4 tbsp vegetable stock
30ml/2 tbsp light soy sauce
15ml/1 tbsp granulated sugar
30ml/2 tbsp rice vinegar
2.5ml/½ tsp dried chilli flakes
small bunch of fresh coriander
    (cilantro), chopped

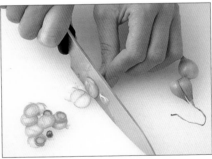

1 Slice the shallots thinly using a sharp knife. Finely chop the garlic.

2 Heat the oil in a wok or large frying pan and cook the shallots and garlic for 2–3 minutes over a medium heat, until golden. Do not let the garlic burn or it will taste bitter.

3 Add the shredded cabbage, toss over the heat for 30 seconds, then add the corn cobs and repeat the process.

4 Add the red peppers, mangetouts and tofu in the same way, each time adding a single ingredient and tossing it over the heat for about 30 seconds before adding the next ingredient.

5 Pour in the stock and soy sauce. Mix together the sugar and vinegar in a small bowl, stirring until the sugar has dissolved, then add to the wok or pan. Sprinkle over the chilli flakes and coriander, toss to mix well and serve.

SPICED TOFU STIR-FRY

Any cooked vegetable could be added to this tasty stir-fry but it is always a good idea to try to achieve a contrast in colours and textures to make the dish more interesting.

SERVES 4

10ml/2 tsp ground cumin
15ml/1 tbsp paprika
5ml/1 tsp ground ginger
good pinch of cayenne pepper
15ml/1 tbsp caster (superfine) sugar
275g/10oz firm tofu
60ml/4 tbsp olive oil
2 garlic cloves, crushed
1 bunch of spring onions
   (scallions), sliced
1 red (bell) pepper, seeded
   and sliced
1 yellow (bell) pepper, seeded
   and sliced
225g/8oz/generous 3 cups brown-cap
   (cremini) mushrooms, halved or
   quartered, if necessary
1 large courgette (zucchini), sliced
115g/4oz fine green beans, halved
50g/2oz/scant ½ cup pine nuts
15ml/1 tbsp lime juice
15ml/1 tbsp maple syrup
salt and ground black pepper

1 Mix together the ground cumin, paprika, ginger, cayenne and sugar in a bowl and season with plenty of salt and pepper. Cut the tofu into cubes with a sharp knife and gently toss the cubes in the spice mixture to coat.

2 Heat half the olive oil in a wok or large, heavy frying pan. Add the tofu cubes and cook over a high heat for 3–4 minutes, turning occasionally (take care not to break up the tofu too much). Remove with a slotted spoon and set aside. Wipe out the wok or pan with kitchen paper.

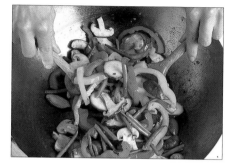

3 Add the remaining oil to the wok or pan and cook the garlic and spring onions for 3 minutes. Add the remaining vegetables and cook over a medium heat for 6 minutes, or until they are beginning to soften and turn golden. Season well.

4 Return the tofu cubes to the wok or frying pan and add the pine nuts, lime juice and maple syrup. Heat through gently, stirring occasionally, for a few minutes, then transfer to warm serving bowls and serve immediately.

TERIYAKI SOBA NOODLES with TOFU and ASPARAGUS

Japanese soba noodles are made from buckwheat flour, which gives them a unique texture and colour. Here they are combined with tofu and asparagus and flavoured with a home-made teriyaki sauce.

SERVES 4

350g/12oz soba noodles
30ml/2 tbsp toasted sesame oil
½ bunch asparagus tips
30ml/2 tbsp groundnut (peanut) oil
250g/9oz firm tofu
2 spring onions (scallions), cut diagonally
1 carrot, cut into thin batons
2.5ml/½ tsp chilli flakes
15ml/1 tbsp sesame seeds
salt and ground black pepper

For the teriyaki sauce
60ml/4 tbsp dark soy sauce
60ml/4 tbsp sake (Japanese rice wine)
60ml/4 tbsp mirin (sweet rice wine)
5ml/1 tsp sugar

1 Cook the noodles according to the instructions on the packet, then drain and rinse under cold running water. Set aside until required.

2 Heat the sesame oil in a griddle pan or on a baking tray placed under the grill (broiler) until very hot. Turn down the heat to medium, then cook the asparagus for 8–10 minutes, turning frequently, until tender and lightly browned. Set aside.

COOK'S TIP
Sesame seeds are an excellent source of the antioxidant vitamin E, which acts as a natural preservative, preventing oxidation and strengthening the heart and nerves.

3 Meanwhile, heat the groundnut oil in a wok or large frying pan until very hot. Add the block of tofu and cook for 8–10 minutes until golden, turning it occasionally to crisp all sides. Carefully remove from the wok or pan and leave to drain on kitchen paper. Cut the tofu into 1cm/½in slices.

4 To prepare the teriyaki sauce, mix the soy sauce, sake or dry sherry, mirin and sugar together, then heat the mixture in the wok or frying pan.

5 Toss in the noodles and stir to coat them in the sauce. Heat through for 1–2 minutes, then spoon into warmed individual serving bowls with the tofu slices and asparagus. Sprinkle the spring onions and carrot on top and then sprinkle with the chilli flakes and sesame seeds. Serve immediately.

VARIATION
Use dried egg or rice noodles instead of soba noodles, if you like.

INDIAN MEE GORENG

This is a truly international recipe that combines Indian, Chinese and Western ingredients into one flavoursome dish. It is a delicious treat for lunch or supper, and quick and easy to prepare too.

SERVES 4–6

450g/1lb fresh yellow egg noodles
60–90ml/4–6 tbsp vegetable oil
115g/4oz marinated deep-fried tofu
2 eggs
30ml/2 tbsp water
1 onion, sliced
1 garlic clove, crushed
15ml/1 tbsp light soy sauce
30–45ml/2–3 tbsp tomato ketchup
15ml/1 tbsp chilli sauce
1 large cooked potato, diced
4 spring onions (scallions), shredded
1–2 fresh green chillies, seeded and thinly
    sliced (optional)

1 Bring a large pan of water to the boil, add the fresh egg noodles and cook for just 2 minutes. Drain the noodles and immediately rinse them under cold water to halt any further cooking. Drain again and set aside.

2 Cut each cube of fried tofu in half with a sharp knife, refresh it in a pan of boiling water, then drain well. Heat 30ml/2 tbsp of the vegetable oil in a large, heavy frying pan.

3 Beat the eggs with the water and seasoning. Add to the pan and cook, until set. Flip over, cook the other side, then slide it out of the pan and roll up.

4 Heat the remaining oil in a large wok and stir-fry the onion and garlic for 2–3 minutes. Add the noodles, soy sauce, ketchup and chilli sauce. Toss over a medium heat for 2 minutes, then add the diced potato.

5 Reserve a few spring onions for the garnish and stir the rest into the noodles with the chilli, if using, and the tofu. Thinly slice the omelette and stir into the mixture. Serve on a hot platter garnished with spring onions.

VARIATION
You can use plain firm tofu instead of fried tofu. Cut it into cubes and fry until brown, then lift out with a slotted spoon.

VEGETABLE and MARINATED TOFU PASTA

This recipe is endlessly versatile. Feel inspired to change it to suit the ingredients you have to hand – the more colourful, the better. Make sure that you chop all the vegetables into even-size pieces so that they all cook by the same time.

SERVES 4

4 carrots, halved lengthways and thinly
    sliced diagonally
1 butternut squash, peeled, seeded and cut
    into small chunks
2 courgettes (zucchini), thinly
    sliced diagonally
1 red onion, cut into wedges
1 red (bell) pepper, seeded and sliced into
    thick strips
1 garlic bulb, cut in half horizontally
leaves from 4 fresh rosemary or thyme
    sprigs (optional)
60ml/4 tbsp olive oil
60ml/4 tbsp balsamic vinegar
30ml/2 tbsp soy sauce
500g/1¼lb marinated deep-fried tofu
10–12 cherry tomatoes, halved
250g/9oz dried pasta, such as papardelle,
    fusilli or conchiglie
sea salt and ground black pepper

1 Preheat the oven to 220°C/425°F/ Gas 7. Place the carrots, butternut squash, courgettes, onion wedges and pepper in a large, deep roasting pan, spreading them out well. Add the garlic, cut side down, and herb sprigs. Drizzle over the olive oil, balsamic vinegar and soy sauce.

2 Season to taste with sea salt and pepper and toss to mix together and coat evenly with the oil. Roast the vegetables for 50–60 minutes, until they are tender and lightly browned at the edges. Toss the vegetables around once or twice during the cooking to expose different sides and cook evenly.

3 Add the tofu and cherry tomatoes to the roasting pan 10 minutes before the end of the roasting time. Meanwhile, bring a large pan of lightly salted water to the boil, add the pasta, bring back to the boil and cook for 10 minutes or until *al dente*. Drain the pasta and return to the pan with a few tablespoons of the cooking water.

4 Remove the roasting pan from the oven and squeeze the garlic out of the baked skins using a wooden spoon. Toss the pasta with the vegetables, tofu and garlic, taste and adjust the seasoning, if necessary, and serve immediately.

COOK'S TIP
When cooking pasta, start timing as soon as the water returns to the boil – and boil fairly vigorously, don't simmer. Test shortly before the end of the cooking time by biting a small piece of pasta between your front teeth, It should feel tender, but still firm to the bite – *al dente*, meaning "to the tooth".

VARIATIONS
Other vegetables that are lovely roasted include beetroot (beet) and celeriac.

NASI GORENG

Serve this Indonesian fried rice dish with the traditional salad called acar bening, *which comprises half a chopped cucumber, two or three chopped pineapple slices, two chopped tomatoes and lime juice and seasoning, including a sprinkling of dried chilli flakes.*

SERVES 4

15ml/1 tbsp Indonesian or Thai red
   curry paste
60ml/4 tbsp soy sauce
250g/9oz firm tofu, drained
250g/9oz/generous 1¼ cups Thai fragrant
   or basmati rice
30ml/2 tbsp groundnut (peanut) oil
2 garlic cloves, finely chopped
1 bunch of spring onions (scallions), thinly
   sliced diagonally
90g/3½oz green beans, thinly sliced
200g/7oz/1¾ cups frozen peas
3 eggs, lightly beaten
50g/2oz/scant 1 cup desiccated
   (dry unsweetened shredded)
   coconut, toasted
50g/2oz/½ cup peanuts, roasted
   and chopped
small bunch of fresh coriander
   (cilantro), chopped

1 Whisk the red curry paste and soy sauce together in a bowl and crumble the tofu into it in large chunks. Set aside to marinate until required.

2 Cook the rice according to the instructions on the packet, until tender, then drain. (Don't add salt to Thai fragrant rice.) Meanwhile, heat the oil in a large, non-stick frying pan or wok and stir-fry the garlic and spring onions for 10 minutes, or until softened and golden.

3 Add the beans, tofu and peas and stir-fry for 5 minutes, breaking up the tofu with a spoon. Add the cooked rice and coconut and stir through.

4 Push everything to one side of the pan or wok, then tip the beaten eggs into the space. Stir gently until they set, like scrambled eggs.

5 Stir the eggs into the rice and other ingredients. Sprinkle with the peanuts and chopped coriander, transfer to warm serving bowls and serve immediately.

VARIATIONS
You could use almost any fresh vegetables in this flexible recipe, from courgettes (zucchini), carrots, broccoli or beansprouts to mangetout (snow peas), watercress and Chinese leaves (Chinese cabbage).

TOFU POPOVER

You can, of course, buy vegetarian tofu sausages to make this family favourite, but making them yourself is very easy and they taste simply wonderful.

SERVES 4

For the vegetarian sausages
150g/5oz/2½ cups fresh breadcrumbs
250g/9oz firm tofu, drained
½ small onion, coarsely chopped
10g/¼oz/¼ cup fresh parsley, thyme, sage
   or rosemary, finely chopped or
   10ml/2 tsp dried herbs
5ml/1 tsp Dijon mustard
5ml/1 tsp soy sauce
1 egg

For the onion gravy
30ml/2 tbsp vegetable oil
1kg/2¼lb large onions, thinly sliced
105ml/7 tbsp red or dry white wine
   or water
300ml/½ pint/1¼ cups vegetable stock
small bunch fresh thyme, woody stems
   removed, chopped (optional)

For the batter
120g/4½oz/generous 1 cup plain
   (all-purpose) flour
1 egg
300ml/½ pint/1¼ cups soya milk
sea salt and ground black pepper

1 First, make the vegetarian sausages. Put all the ingredients, together with sea salt and pepper to taste, in a food processor and process to a thick paste. Scrape out the mixture and divide it into eight portions. Roll them into sausage shapes with your hands. The mixture will be slightly wet, but will form the shape quite easily. Put the sausages on a large plate in a single layer, cover with clear film (plastic wrap) and chill in the refrigerator until required.

2 To make the onion gravy, heat the oil in a large non-stick frying pan. Add the onion and cook over a medium heat for 5 minutes, until beginning to turn golden. Reduce the heat to its lowest setting, cover the pan, then cook for 10 minutes, stirring occasionally, until softened and coloured.

3 Add the wine or water and stock and bring to the boil. Simmer, uncovered, for 10 minutes, until reduced and thickened.

4 Meanwhile, preheat the oven to 220°C/425°F/Gas 7. To make the batter, sift the flour into a large bowl and season with salt and pepper. Make a well in the middle, then add the egg and half the soya milk.

5 Gradually stir in the flour until fully incorporated, then beat until smooth. Stir in the remaining soya milk.

6 Oil a shallow ovenproof dish, then arrange the vegetarian sausages in the base in a single layer with a little space between each. Pour in the batter and bake for 40–45 minutes, or until the batter is well risen and brown.

7 Serve the popover cut into portions with two sausages each, and accompanied by the onion gravy.

COOK'S TIP
The vegetarian sausages are also good cooked on their own. To do so, place them on a baking sheet and drizzle with olive oil. Cook under a preheated grill (broiler), turning frequently, for about 10–12 minutes, until golden brown all over and heated through.

POTATO ROSTI and TOFU with FRESH TOMATO and GINGER SAUCE

Although this dish features various components, it is not difficult to make and the finished result is well worth the effort. Make sure you marinate the tofu for at least an hour to allow it to absorb the flavours of the ginger, garlic and tamari. Serve with a mixed leaf salad, dressed with a splash each of toasted sesame oil and lime juice.

SERVES 4

425g/15oz firm tofu, cut into 1cm/
½in cubes
4 large potatoes, about 900g/2lb total
weight, peeled
sunflower oil, for frying
salt and ground black pepper
30ml/2 tbsp sesame seeds, toasted,
to serve

For the marinade
30ml/2 tbsp tamari or dark soy sauce
15ml/1 tbsp clear honey
2 garlic cloves, crushed
4cm/1½in piece fresh root ginger, grated
5ml/1 tsp toasted sesame oil

For the sauce
15ml/1 tbsp olive oil
8 tomatoes, halved, seeded
and chopped

1 Mix together all the marinade ingredients in a shallow dish and add the tofu cubes. Spoon the marinade over the tofu and leave to marinate in the refrigerator for at least 1 hour. Turn the tofu occasionally in the marinade to allow the flavours to infuse (steep).

2 To make the rösti, par-boil the potatoes for 10–15 minutes, until almost tender. Drain well, leave to cool, then grate coarsely. Season to taste with salt and pepper. Preheat the oven to 200°C/400°F/Gas 6.

3 Using a slotted spoon, remove the tofu from the marinade and reserve the marinade. Spread out the tofu on a baking sheet and bake, turning the cubes occasionally with a fish slice or metal spatula, for 20 minutes, until golden and crisp on all sides.

4 Take a quarter of the potato mixture at a time and form into four coarse patties with your hands

5 Heat a frying pan with just enough oil to cover the base. Place the patties in the frying pan and flatten the mixture, using your hands or a spatula to form rounds about 1cm/½in thick.

6 Cook for about 6 minutes, until golden and crisp on the undersides. Carefully turn over the rösti with a fish slice or metal spatula and cook for a further 6 minutes, until golden.

7 Meanwhile, make the sauce. Heat the olive oil in a pan, add the reserved marinade and the tomatoes and cook over a medium heat, stirring constantly, for 2 minutes. Reduce the heat to low, cover and simmer gently, stirring occasionally, for 10 minutes, until the tomatoes break down. Press through a sieve with the back of a wooden spoon to make a thick, smooth sauce.

8 To serve, place a rösti on each of four warmed serving plates. Arrange the tofu cubes on top, spoon over the tomato and ginger sauce and sprinkle with sesame seeds. Serve immediately.

COOK'S TIPS
• If you have time, chill the par-boiled potatoes before grating them, as this makes the task much easier.
• If you are in a hurry, thinly slice one raw potato at a time with a mandolin. Don't rinse, but simply pile the potato into the pan and cook for 45 seconds. Flip over and cook the other side.

VEGETABLE MOUSSAKA with TOFU TOPPING

This Greek dish, traditionally made with lamb and topped with a cheese sauce, has been ingeniously adapted for vegetarians and vegans. It contains no animal products at all, but is still as rich-tasting and full of flavour as the original.

SERVES 8

600g/1lb 5oz aubergines (eggplant), cut into 2.5cm/1in slices
30ml/2 tbsp olive oil
50ml/3½ tbsp water
paprika and fresh basil leaves, to garnish

For the sauce
30ml/2 tbsp olive oil
2 large onions, coarsely chopped
2 garlic cloves, crushed
2 large carrots, finely chopped
4 courgettes (zucchini), sliced
200g/7oz mushrooms, sliced
2 × 400g/14oz cans chopped tomatoes
30ml/2 tbsp balsamic vinegar
5ml/1 tsp Tabasco sauce
15ml/1 tbsp clear honey
sea salt and ground black pepper

For the tofu topping
200g/7oz/1¾ cups ground almonds
350g/12oz silken tofu, drained
15ml/1 tbsp soy sauce
15ml/1 tbsp lemon juice
2.5ml/½ tsp English (hot) mustard powder

1 Preheat the grill (broiler) to high and place the aubergine slices in one layer on the grill rack. Drizzle with olive oil and grill (broil) for 2–3 minutes on each side until lightly browned.

2 To make the sauce, heat the oil in a large pan and sauté the onion, garlic and carrots for 5–7 minutes, until softened. Add the remaining ingredients, bring to the boil, then simmer for 20 minutes, stirring occasionally. Season.

3 Meanwhile make the topping. Toast the ground almonds in a heavy frying pan, without any oil, for 1–2 minutes, tossing occasionally until golden. Reserve 75g/3oz/¾ cup. Tip them into a food processor and add the remaining ingredients. Process until smooth and combined and adjust the seasoning.

4 Preheat the oven to 180°C/350°F/ Gas 4. Spread half the vegetable tomato sauce in the base of a 35 × 23cm/ 14 × 9in deep-sided ovenproof dish. Arrange the aubergine slices on top and spread over the remaining sauce.

5 Add the tofu topping. Sprinkle with the reserved almonds. Bake for 20 minutes until the top is set and browned. Garnish with paprika and basil.

FRIED GARLIC TOFU

A simple and inexpensive recipe that can be quickly and easily prepared to make a tasty and nutritious midweek family supper. In summer, serve with mixed salad leaves or steamed greens and minted new potatoes and, in winter, serve with baked potatoes.

SERVES 4

500g/1¼lb firm tofu
50g/2oz/¼ cup butter
2 garlic cloves, thinly sliced
200g/7oz enoki or other mushrooms
45ml/3 tbsp soy sauce
30ml/2 tbsp sake or lemon juice

1 Wrap the tofu in kitchen paper, place a weighted plate on top and leave for up to 1 hour to drain off excess water.

2 Slice the tofu to make 16 slices using a sharp knife.

3 Melt one-third of the butter in a frying pan. Add the garlic and cook over a medium heat, stirring, until golden, but do not allow it to burn. Remove the garlic from the pan. Add half the remaining butter to the pan, add the mushrooms and cook for 3–4 minutes, until golden and softened, then remove the mushrooms from the pan.

4 Place the tofu in the pan with the remaining butter and cook over a medium heat. Turn over and cook the other side until golden and the tofu is warmed through.

5 Return the garlic to the pan, add the soy sauce and sake or lemon juice and simmer for 1 minute. Transfer to warm serving plates and serve immediately with the mushrooms.

TOFU and GREEN BEAN RED CURRY

One of those versatile recipes that should be in every cook's repertoire. This quick and easy version uses green beans, but other types of vegetable work equally well.

SERVES 4–6

600ml/1 pint/2½ cups canned coconut milk
15ml/1 tbsp Thai red curry paste
45ml/3 tbsp Thai fish sauce
    (see Cook's Tip)
10ml/2 tsp palm sugar or light muscovado
    (brown) sugar
225g/8oz/3¼ cups button
    (white) mushrooms
115g/4oz/scant 1 cup green beans
175g/6oz firm tofu, rinsed, drained and cut
    in 2cm/¾in cubes
4 kaffir lime leaves, torn
2 fresh red chillies, seeded and sliced
fresh coriander (cilantro) leaves, to garnish

COOK'S TIP
Thai fish sauce, also known as *nam pla*, is widely available from supermarkets.

1 Pour about one-third of the coconut milk into a wok or pan. Cook until it starts to separate and an oily sheen appears on the surface.

2 Add the red curry paste, fish sauce and sugar to the coconut milk. Mix thoroughly, then add the mushrooms. Stir and cook for 1 minute.

3 Stir in the remaining coconut milk. Bring back to the boil, then add the green beans and tofu cubes. Simmer gently for 4–5 minutes more.

4 Stir in the kaffir lime leaves and sliced red chillies. Spoon the curry into a serving dish, garnish with the coriander leaves and serve immediately.

TOFU BALLS with SPAGHETTI

*This dish makes a great family supper, as children and adults alike really love the little
tofu balls and the rich vegetable sauce, while pasta never fails to please.*

SERVES 4

250g/9oz firm tofu, drained
1 onion, coarsely grated
2 garlic cloves, crushed
5ml/1 tsp Dijon mustard
15ml/1 tbsp ground cumin
1 small bunch of parsley,
   finely chopped
15ml/1 tbsp soy sauce
50g/2oz/½ cup ground almonds
30ml/2 tbsp olive oil
350g/12oz spaghetti
sea salt and ground black pepper

For the sauce
15ml/1 tbsp olive oil
1 large onion, finely chopped
2 garlic cloves, chopped
1 large aubergine (eggplant), diced
2 courgettes (zucchini), diced
1 red (bell) pepper, seeded and
   finely chopped
pinch of sugar
400g/14oz can chopped tomatoes
200ml/7fl oz/scant 1 cup vegetable stock
1 bunch of fresh basil

1 Place the drained tofu, grated onion, crushed garlic, mustard, ground cumin, chopped parsley, soy sauce and ground almonds into a bowl. Season well with sea salt and ground black pepper and mix thoroughly. Roll into about 20 walnut-sized balls, squashing the mixture together with your hands.

2 Heat the olive oil in a large frying pan, then cook the balls, turning them gently until brown all over. Remove from the pan and set aside on a plate.

3 Heat the oil for the sauce in the same frying pan, add the onion and garlic and cook for 5 minutes, or until softened.

4 Add the aubergine, courgette, pepper, sugar and seasoning and stir-fry for 10 minutes until the vegetables are beginning to soften and brown.

5 Stir in the tomatoes and stock. Cover and simmer for 20–30 minutes, or until the sauce is rich and thickened. Just before the end of the cooking time, place the tofu balls gently on top of the sauce, replace the lid and heat through for 2–3 minutes.

6 Meanwhile, cook the pasta in large pan of salted, boiling water according to the manufacturer's instructions, then drain. Sprinkle the sauce with the basil and check the seasoning before serving with the spaghetti.

COOK'S TIP
This vegetable sauce will stand on its own as a sauce for meat or fish or as a filling for baked potatoes.

TOFU and VEGETABLE THAI CURRY

Traditional Thai ingredients – coconut milk, chillies, galangal, lemon grass and kaffir lime
leaves – give this curry a wonderfully fragrant aroma and a rich flavour.

SERVES 4

175g/6oz firm tofu, drained
45ml/3 tbsp dark soy sauce
15ml/1 tbsp sesame oil
5ml/1 tsp chilli sauce
2.5cm/1in piece fresh root ginger,
 finely grated
225g/8oz cauliflower
225g/8oz broccoli
30ml/2 tbsp vegetable oil
1 onion, sliced
400ml/14fl oz/1⅔ cups coconut milk
150ml/¼ pint/⅔ cup water
1 red (bell) pepper, seeded and chopped
175g/6oz green beans, halved
115g/4oz/1½ cups shiitake or button
 (white) mushrooms, halved
shredded spring onions (scallions),
 to garnish
boiled Thai fragrant rice or noodles,
 to serve

For the curry paste
2 fresh green chillies, seeded
 and chopped
1 lemon grass stalk, chopped
2.5cm/1in piece fresh galangal, chopped
2 kaffir lime leaves
10ml/2 tsp ground coriander
a few sprigs fresh coriander (cilantro),
 including the stalks

1 Cut the drained tofu into 2.5cm/1in cubes and place in an ovenproof dish. Mix together the soy sauce, sesame oil, chilli sauce and ginger and pour over the tofu. Toss gently to coat all the cubes evenly, then leave to marinate for at least 4 hours or overnight if possible, turning and basting the tofu occasionally.

2 To make the curry paste, place the chopped chillies, lemon grass, galangal, kaffir lime leaves, ground coriander and fresh coriander in a food processor and process for a few seconds until well blended. Add 45ml/3 tbsp water and process to a thick paste.

3 Preheat the oven to 190°C/375°F/ Gas 5. Using a large sharp knife, cut the cauliflower and broccoli into small florets and cut any stalks into thin slices.

4 Heat the vegetable oil in a frying pan, add the sliced onion and cook gently for about 8 minutes, or until soft and lightly browned. Stir in the prepared curry paste and the coconut milk. Add the water and bring to the boil.

5 Stir in the red pepper, green beans, cauliflower and broccoli. Transfer to a Chinese sand pot or earthenware casserole. Cover and place in the oven.

6 Stir the tofu and marinade, then place the dish in the top of the oven and cook for 30 minutes, then stir them into the curry with the mushrooms. Reduce the oven temperature to 180°C/350°F/Gas 4 and cook for about 15 minutes, or until the vegetables are tender. Garnish with spring onions and serve with boiled Thai fragrant rice or noodles.

COOK'S TIP
Thai fragrant rice is also known as jasmine rice. Before cooking, rinse it at least three times in cold water until the water runs clear. Place it in a large pan and add 750ml/1¼ pints/3 cups cold water for every 450g/1lb/2 cups rice. Bring to a vigorous boil over a high heat, then stir and reduce the heat to low. Cover and simmer for 15–20 minutes, until all the water has been absorbed. Remove from the heat and leave to stand, still covered, for 10 minutes. Remove the lid and gently stir the rice with a fork or chopsticks to fluff up the grains.

MEAT, CHICKEN AND FISH DISHES

This fabulous collection of mouthwatering recipes cannot fail to convince you that tofu is not just for vegetarians. Combining tofu with meat, poultry, chicken and seafood gives you the best of both worlds – all your favourite flavours but with far less fat. Tofu provides a delicious contrast to the other ingredients, whether it's cooked with the meat, poultry or fish, or incorporated in a rich-tasting creamy sauce.

MONGOLIAN FIREPOT

This mode of cooking was introduced to China by the Mongols in the 13th century. Guests cook the ingredients at the table, dipping the meats in a variety of sauces, then a soup is made with the stock and Chinese leaves, spinach, tofu and noodles.

SERVES 6–8

900g/2lb boned leg of lamb, preferably bought thinly sliced
225g/8oz lamb's liver and/or kidneys
900ml/1½ pints/3¾ cups lamb stock (see Cook's Tip)
900ml/1½ pints/3¾ cups chicken stock
1cm/½in piece fresh root ginger, thinly sliced
45ml/3 tbsp rice wine or medium dry sherry
½ head Chinese leaves (Chinese cabbage), shredded
few young spinach leaves
250g/9oz firm tofu, diced
115g/4oz cellophane noodles
salt and ground black pepper

For the dipping sauce
50ml/2fl oz/¼ cup red wine vinegar
7.5ml/½ tbsp dark soy sauce
1cm/½in piece fresh root ginger, finely shredded
1 spring onion (scallion), finely shredded

To serve
crusty bread
bowls of tomato sauce, sweet chilli sauce, mustard oil and sesame oil
dry-fried coriander seeds, crushed

1 Ask your butcher to slice the lamb thinly on a slicing machine, if possible. If you have had to buy it in a piece, however, put it in the freezer for about an hour, so that it is easier to slice thinly.

COOK'S TIP
When buying the lamb, ask the butcher for the bones and make your own lamb stock. Rinse the bones and place them in a large pan with enough water to cover. Bring to the boil and skim the surface well. Add 1 peeled onion, 2 peeled carrots, 1cm/½in piece of peeled and bruised ginger, 5ml/1 tsp salt and ground black pepper to taste. Bring back to the boil, then simmer for about 1 hour until the stock is full of flavour. Strain, leave to cool, then skim and use.

2 Trim the liver and remove the skin and core from the kidneys, if using. Place them in the freezer too. If you managed to buy sliced lamb, keep it in the refrigerator until needed.

3 Mix both types of stock in a large pan. Add the sliced ginger and rice wine or sherry and season with salt and pepper to taste. Heat to simmering point and simmer for 15 minutes.

4 Slice all the meats thinly and arrange them attractively on a large platter.

5 Place the Chinese leaves, spinach and the tofu on a platter. Soak the noodles, following the instructions on the packet.

6 Make the dipping sauce by mixing all the ingredients in a small bowl. The other sauces and the crushed coriander seeds should be spooned into separate small dishes and placed on a serving tray. Have ready a basket of freshly steamed flower rolls.

7 Fill the moat of the hotpot with the simmering stock. Alternatively, fill a fondue pot and place it over a burner. Each guest selects a portion of meat from the platter and cooks it in the hot stock, using chopsticks or a fondue fork. The meat is then dipped in one of the sauces and coated with the coriander seeds (if liked) before being eaten with a chunk of crusty bread.

8 When all or most of the meat has been cooked and eaten, top up the stock, if necessary, then add the Chinese leaves, spinach leaves, tofu and drained noodles. Cook for 1–2 minutes, until the noodles are tender and the vegetables are cooked, but retain a little crispness. Ladle the soup into warmed bowls and serve with any remaining crusty bread.

SUKIYAKI

Thin slices of tender, marinated beef, tofu and vegetables are fried and then simmered in a sweet stock at the table in this Japanese dish. They are then dipped in a delicious ginger and mustard marinade before they are eaten.

SERVES 4–6

450g/1lb fillet steak (beef tenderloin)
250g/9oz firm tofu, cut into 1cm/½in cubes
200g/7oz sugar snap peas
1 bunch purple spring onions (scallions),
    sliced diagonally into 2.5cm/1in pieces
juice of 1 lime
bunch of coriander (cilantro), chopped
lime wedges and boiled rice, to serve

For the marinade
2.5cm/1in piece fresh root ginger, chopped
1 garlic clove, crushed
15ml/1 tbsp wholegrain mustard
60ml/4 tbsp soy sauce
15ml/1 tbsp sesame oil

For the warishita stock
30ml/2 tbsp brown sugar
45ml/3 tbsp mirin (sweet rice wine)
100ml/3½fl oz/scant ½ cup soy sauce
100ml/3½fl oz/scant ½ cup
    vegetable stock

1 Place the fillet steak between two pieces of baking parchment and beat out with a meat mallet or a rolling pin until evenly thin. Cut into 2.5cm/1in wide, bitesize strips.

2 Place all the marinade ingredients in a large dish and mix together well. Add the steak strips and tofu cubes and toss together until thoroughly coated. Set aside. Mix all the warishita stock ingredients together in a bowl or jug (pitcher) until thoroughly combined.

3 Heat a small wok until very hot, then transfer to a burner at the table. Add the steak and tofu and cook for a few seconds on each side. Add the warishita stock and the vegetables and cook for a few minutes, or until tender, then add the lime juice and coriander. Spoon the marinade into individual dipping saucers.

4 Diners help themselves from the wok and eat the sukiyaki dipped in the marinade and served with lime wedges and boiled rice.

SICHUAN BEEF with TOFU

China's western province is famous for its spicy cuisine, full of strong flavours. Sichuan peppercorns, which feature in this meat dish are not, in fact, peppercorns, but the dried berries of a type of ash tree. But, they do have a very peppery flavour.

SERVES 4

200g/7oz/1 cup Thai fragrant or
    basmati rice
30ml/2 tbsp groundnut (peanut) or soya oil
4 garlic cloves, finely chopped
600g/1lb 6oz beef steak, cut into
    thin strips
500g/1¼lb firm tofu, drained and diced
1 head broccoli, coarsely chopped
90ml/6 tbsp soy sauce
pinch of sugar
juice of 1 lime
ground Sichuan peppercorns
sweet chilli sauce, to
    serve (optional)

1 Cook the rice in salted boiling water until tender, according to the instructions on the packet, then set aside.

2 Heat the oil in a large non-stick wok or frying pan, then add the garlic and stir-fry for a few seconds, until golden. Increase the heat to high, add the strips of steak and stir-fry briefly to seal.

3 Add the tofu cubes and broccoli and stir-fry for a few seconds. Stir in the soy sauce, sugar, lime juice and ground Sichuan peppercorns, then stir-fry for about 2 minutes. Transfer to warm serving plates or bowls and serve immediately with the rice and chilli sauce, if you like.

PORK and TOFU CROQUETTES

Combining pork and tofu in these tasty, deep-fried croquettes not only helps to eke out the meat, but also minimizes the quantity of saturated fat – economical and healthy.

2 Heat a little vegetable oil in a large frying pan, then add the pork, onion, mustard, thyme or sage and seasoning. Stir fry for 5–10 minutes, until the pork is cooked and golden.

3 Add the pork mixture to the tofu and divide into eight equal-size portions.

4 Shape each portion into a croquette shape, then coat first in flour, then egg and, finally, breadcrumbs.

5 Heat the oil for deep-frying to 180–190°C/350–375°F or until a cube of day-old bread browns in 30 seconds. Deep-fry the croquettes until golden, then drain on kitchen paper. Serve with sweet chilli sauce or ketchup, if you like.

SERVES 4

250g/9oz firm tofu
150g/5oz/1¼ cups minced
    (ground) pork
½ onion, finely chopped
10ml/2 tsp English (hot) mustard
5ml/1 tsp finely chopped fresh thyme
    or sage
plain (all-purpose) flour, for coating
2 eggs, beaten
90g/3½oz/1¾ cups fresh breadcrumbs
vegetable oil, for deep-frying
sea salt and ground black pepper
sweet chilli sauce or tomato ketchup, to
    serve (optional)

1 Drain the tofu, then wrap it in a dishtowel or kitchen paper and place a weighted plate on top. Leave for up to 1 hour to remove any excess water, then place the tofu in a bowl and mash.

THAI CURRY with CHICKEN and TOFU

This delicious Thai curry is highly flavoured and hot. Serve with plain rice and either some steamed green beans or broccoli, or pak choi with a sprinkling of soy sauce.

SERVES 4

30ml/2 tbsp groundnut (peanut) or soya oil
2 garlic cloves, crushed
2 onions, chopped
2.5cm/1in piece fresh root ginger,
   finely chopped
4 skinless chicken fillets, each weighing
   about 150g/5oz, chopped into
   bitesize pieces
15–30ml/1–2 tbsp Thai green or red curry
   paste (see Cook's Tips)
45ml/3 tbsp soy sauce
150g/5oz marinated deep-fried tofu
grated rind and juice of 1 lime
120ml/4fl oz/½ cup chicken stock
pinch of sugar
90g/3½oz watercress
20g/¾oz fresh coriander (cilantro), chopped
400ml/14fl oz/1⅔ cups coconut milk
30ml/2 tbsp peanuts, toasted and chopped,
   to garnish

1 Heat the oil in a non-stick wok or large frying pan, then stir-fry the garlic, onion and ginger for 4–5 minutes, until golden brown and softened.

2 Add the chicken pieces and stir-fry for 2–3 minutes, until browned all over. Add the curry paste and stir to coat the chicken. Add the soy sauce, tofu, grated lime rind and juice, the stock and sugar, and stir-fry for 2 minutes.

VARIATION
Vary the vegetables used to suit the season and your taste – mangetouts (snow peas), baby corn, courgettes (zucchini), carrots, broccoli florets and green beans all work well.

3 Add the watercress and coriander, reserving a little for the garnish, and stir-fry for a further 2 minutes. Add the coconut milk and heat through gently, stirring occasionally, but do not allow to come to the boil.

4 Taste and adjust the seasoning, if necessary, then serve garnished with the peanuts and reserved coriander.

COOK'S TIP
Thai curry paste is very hot, so if you haven't used it before – beware. Most people find 5ml/1 tsp enough to give the fragrant flavours without too much heat but if you are used to hot food, then increase the amount to 10ml/2 tsp. Both red and green curry pastes – made with red and green chillies respectively – are available from most supermarkets and from Asian food stores.

SEAFOOD and TOFU PAELLA

Not exactly authentic, but given that there are as many versions of paella as there are cooks in Spain, why not enjoy an easy and inexpensive tofu version of this tasty dish?

SERVES 4

pinch of saffron threads
30ml/2 tbsp boiling water
15ml/1 tbsp vegetable oil
1 garlic clove, crushed
1 red (bell) pepper, seeded
   and diced
2–3 ripe tomatoes, coarsely chopped
1.5ml/¼ tsp paprika or cayenne pepper
10g/¼oz thyme, woody stems removed,
   the rest chopped
200g/7oz/1 cup long grain or
   basmati rice
50ml/2fl oz/¼ cup dry white wine
600ml/1 pint/2½ cups chicken stock
grated rind and juice of ½ lemon
1 bay leaf
225g/8oz small courgettes (zucchini) or
   patty pan squashes
150g/5oz/1¼ cups fresh or frozen peas
1 bunch of spring onions
   (scallions), chopped
225g/8oz cooked frozen seafood
250g/9oz firm tofu, cut into cubes
sea salt and ground black pepper
lemon wedges, to serve (optional)

1 Place the saffron in a small bowl and add the boiling water. Set aside to soak for 5 minutes.

VARIATIONS
• Leave out the seafood and add more summer vegetables, such as green beans. or broad (fava) beans, for a vegan dish.
• Substitute skinless, boneless chicken breast portions or thighs for the seafood. Dice the meat into even-size pieces and stir-fry with the garlic and red (bell) pepper in step 2.

2 Heat the oil in a large, non-stick frying pan or wok, add the garlic and red pepper and stir-fry over a medium heat for 6–8 minutes, or until the garlic is golden and the pepper softened.

3 Add the tomatoes, saffron and its soaking water, paprika or cayenne pepper, thyme, rice, wine, stock, grated lemon rind and juice and bay leaf and season to taste with salt and pepper. Stir together to mix well. Bring to the boil, lower the heat, cover and simmer gently, for 10 minutes.

4 Meanwhile, using a sharp knife, slice the courgettes or patty pan squashes on the diagonal into even-size pieces about 3mm/⅛in thick.

5 Stir the rice mixture, then pile the courgettes or patty pan squashes, peas, spring onions, seafood and tofu on top of it. Replace the lid and cook for 10 minutes, then uncover and gently fold together, scraping any crusty residue from the base of the pan or wok.

6 Taste and adjust the seasoning, if necessary, and serve immediately with lemon wedges, if you like.

COOK'S TIP
Saffron has a strong, slightly bitter flavour and a powerful fragrance. It is also what gives paella its characteristic golden colour. It is the world's most expensive spice, but there is no substitute. Made from the stigmas of a purple-flowering crocus, it takes 250,000 flowers – which are hand picked – to produce 450g/1lb saffron, so its cost is not surprising. Fortunately, you need only a little to flavour food. The best saffron comes from La Mancha in Spain, but it is also produced in North Africa, India and Iran. Saffron is available as a powder or in threads, but the powder is sometimes mixed with other, cheaper spices.

SALMON with LEMON and TOFU SAUCE

The elegant simplicity of this dish makes it an ideal choice for a dinner party. Moreover, it is very quick and easy to prepare while looking and tasting wonderful. You could also serve other fish, such as sea trout, with the same creamy textured sauce.

SERVES 2

2 salmon steaks or fillets, each weighing about 130–150g/4½–5oz
5cm/2in piece fresh root ginger, cut into thin sticks
2 garlic cloves, finely chopped
1 small red chilli, seeded and finely chopped
bunch of fresh dill, parsley or coriander (cilantro), tough stems removed
sea salt and ground black pepper
15ml/1 tbsp sesame seeds, toasted, to garnish

For the sauce
175g/6oz silken tofu
grated rind and juice of 1 lemon
50ml/3½ tbsp water

1 Line a bamboo steaming basket or metal steaming tray with baking parchment, then arrange the salmon steaks or fillets on top. Pile the ginger, garlic and chilli, and half of the dill, parsley or coriander, on top of the fish and season with salt and pepper, then cover and steam for 5–10 minutes, or until the fish is opaque and just cooked through.

2 Meanwhile, make the sauce by blending all the ingredients and the remaining herbs in a blender or food processor until smooth. Transfer to a small pan and gently warm through, stirring frequently.

3 Serve the fish with the sauce spooned over the top and garnished with the toasted sesame seeds.

TOFU, FISH CAKES and VEGETABLES

This Japanese dish, called oden, *is a satisfying and easy one to make at home as you can buy assorted ready-made fish balls and fish cakes from Asian food stores. You will also need a large clay pot or a heavy flameproof casserole and a portable cooker.*

SERVES 4

30 × 7.5cm/12 × 3in dashi-konbu
675g/1½lb mooli (daikon), peeled and cut
    into 4cm/1½in lengths
12–20 ready-made fish balls and cakes
    (buy 3 or 4 different kinds, if you can)
250g/9oz packet konnyaku (see Cook's Tip)
1 atsu-age, cut into pieces
8 small shiitake mushrooms,
    stalks removed
4 potatoes, unpeeled, soaked in a bowl
    of water (to remove some of
    the starch)
4 hard-boiled eggs, unshelled
300g/11oz firm tofu, cut into
    8 cubes
English (hot) mustard, to serve

For the soup stock
1.5 litres/2½ pints/6¼ cups water and
    10ml/2 tsp dashi-no-moto (Japanese
    stock granules)
75ml/5 tbsp Japanese sake
15ml/1 tbsp salt
40ml/8 tsp shoyu

1 Wrap the dashi-konbu in a wet dishtowel for 5 minutes, or until it is soft enough to bend by hand. Snip it in half crossways with kitchen scissors, then cut each piece into four ribbons lengthways. Tie the centre of each ribbon.

2 Slightly shave the edges of each of the mooli cylinders with a small, sharp knife. Place all the fish balls, fish cakes, konnyaku and atsu-age in a large pan. Add enough hot water to cover all the ingredients, then drain.

3 Cut the konnyaku in quarters, then cut each quarter in half diagonally to make eight triangles. Cut large fish cakes in half. Put two shiitake mushrooms on to each of four bamboo skewers.

COOK'S TIP
Konnyaku is a gelatinous cake made from flour that is produced from the root of a plant called the devil's tongue or konjac. It comes in both black and white and is available from Japanese food stores.

4 Mix all the ingredients for the soup stock, but only fill the pot by two-thirds. Add the mooli and potatoes and bring to the boil. Add the hard-boiled eggs. Reduce the heat to low and simmer for 1 hour, uncovered, skimming occasionally.

5 Increase the heat to medium and add the other ingredients. Cover and cook for 30 minutes, then bring the pot to the table cooker and keep warm on the lowest heat. Serve with mustard. Top up the pot with stock if necessary.

DESSERTS

At first sight, these fabulous, utterly scrumptious desserts look really self-indulgent, but they are far from being packed with calories and cream. There are clever tofu versions of everyone's favourites, from Chocolate Mousse to Strawberry and Vanilla Tofu Ice – perfect for family meals and special enough for guests. It just goes to show that you can have your Carrot Cake and eat it too.

MANGO and COCONUT TOFU WHIP

This deliciously smooth dessert has a truly tropical taste. Few fruits are quite so luscious and sweet as mangoes and their slightly resinous flavour is superbly complemented by coconut cream. Add the magical texture of silken tofu and you have perfection in a glass.

SERVES 6

2 large ripe mangoes
200ml/7fl oz/scant 1 cup coconut cream
200g/7oz silken tofu
45ml/3 tbsp maple syrup
mint sprigs or grated lime rind,
   to decorate

COOK'S TIP
Make sure that you buy pure maple syrup for the best flavour.

VARIATION
Try using papaya, banana or raspberries instead of the mango.

1 Using a sharp knife, peel and stone (pit) the mangoes and coarsely chop the flesh. Place the flesh in a blender or food processor with the coconut cream and silken tofu.

2 Add the maple syrup and process to a smooth, rich cream. Pour into serving glasses or bowls and chill for at least 1 hour before serving. Decorate with mint sprigs or some grated lime rind.

DATE and TOFU ICE

This creamy date and apple ice cream is generously spiced with cinnamon and not only does it taste good but is also packed with soya protein, contains no added sugar, is low in fat and free from all dairy products.

SERVES 4

250g/9oz/1½ cups stoned (pitted) dates
600ml/1 pint/2½ cups apple juice
5ml/1 tsp ground cinnamon
300g/11oz firm tofu, drained
   and cubed
150ml/¼ pint/⅔ cup unsweetened
   soya milk

1 Put the dates in a pan. Pour in 300ml/½ pint/1¼ cups of the apple juice and leave to soak for 4 hours. Simmer for 10 minutes, then leave to cool. Using a slotted spoon, lift out one-quarter of the dates, chop coarsely and set aside.

2 Put the remaining dates in a food processor or blender and process to a purée. Add the cinnamon and process with enough of the remaining apple juice to make a smooth paste.

3 Add the cubes of tofu, a few at a time, processing after each addition. Finally, add the remaining apple juice and the soya milk.

4 By hand: Pour the mixture into a plastic tub or similar freezerproof container and freeze for 4 hours, beating once with a fork, electric mixer or in a food processor to break up the ice crystals. After this time, beat well again with a fork to make sure that the texture is completely smooth.
Using an ice cream maker: Churn the mixture until very thick, but not thick enough to scoop. Scrape into a plastic tub with a lid.

5 Stir in some of the chopped dates and freeze for 2–3 hours, until firm.

6 Place scoops of the ice in four dessert glasses and decorate with the remaining chopped dates before serving.

COOK'S TIP
As tofu is a non-dairy product it will not blend completely, so don't be concerned if the mixture contains tiny flecks of tofu.

STRAWBERRY and VANILLA TOFU ICE

This pretty pink dairy-free ice has a remarkably creamy taste. Serve with slices of fresh strawberry, or in a cone, drizzled with strawberry syrup.

2 When the mixture is thick enough to coat the back of the spoon, pour it into a bowl. Remove and discard the vanilla pod. Cover the surface with a sheet of greaseproof (waxed) paper to prevent a skin forming, then leave to cool.

3 Process the tofu, oil, maple syrup and strawberries in a food processor or blender until smooth and creamy.

SERVES 8

450ml/¾ pint/scant 2 cups soya milk
50g/2oz/¼ cup caster
   (superfine) sugar
20ml/4 tsp cornflour (cornstarch)
5ml/1 tsp vanilla essence (extract) or
   1 vanilla pod (bean)
500g/1¼lb silken tofu
15ml/1 tbsp sunflower oil
30ml/2 tbsp maple syrup
250g/9oz/2 cups strawberries, hulled and
   halved, plus extra to decorate

VARIATION

If you like, you can substitute raspberries for the strawberries. Alternatively, you could use peeled, stoned (pitted) and chopped mango or peach.

1 Reserve 60ml/4 tbsp soya milk, then pour the remainder into a large pan and bring to the boil over a medium heat. Blend the sugar and cornflour with the reserved milk in a bowl. Add the sugar mixture and vanilla essence or vanilla pod to the warm milk. Simmer, stirring constantly, for 2 minutes, until thickened.

4 Mix the strawberry mixture into the custard, pour into a freezerproof container and freeze for 2 hours. Whisk the half-frozen mixture until smooth, then return to the freezer for 1 hour. Whisk again and freeze until solid. Remove the ice from the freezer 20 minutes before serving to soften.

TOFU BERRY CHEESECAKE

A glorious fake, this cheesecake does not contain cheese, but no one will be able to tell.
Instead, it owes its wonderful texture to a mixture of tofu and yogurt.

SERVES SIX

425g/15oz firm tofu
300g/11oz sheep's milk yogurt
25ml/1½ tbsp/1½ sachets
    powdered gelatine
90ml/6 tbsp apple juice
175g/6oz/1¾ cups soft fruit, such
    as raspberries, strawberries
    and blueberries
30ml/2 tbsp redcurrant jelly
30ml/2 tbsp hot water

For the base

50g/2oz/¼ cup dairy-free, low-fat spread
    or margarine
30ml/2 tbsp apple juice
115g/4oz/6 cups bran flakes

1 To make the base, place the low-fat spread or margarine and apple juice in a pan and heat them gently until the spread or margarine has melted. Crush the bran flakes and stir them into the apple juice mixture.

2 Tip the mixture into a 23cm/9in loose-based round flan tin (pie pan) and press down firmly with your fingers. Leave base to cool, then chill until set.

COOK'S TIPS
• If the apple juice and bran flakes mixture sticks to your fingers and keeps coming away from the tin (pan) while you are trying to press it flat, try using the base of a clean jar instead.
• Use the same jar to remove the flan from the tin. Stand the base on the inverted jar and carefully slide off the ring part of the tin downwards.

3 To make the filling, place the tofu and yogurt in a food processor and process them until smooth. Soak the gelatine in the apple juice, then heat to dissolve. Stir into the tofu mixture.

4 Spread the tofu mixture over the base, smoothing it evenly. Chill for 1–2 hours, until the filling has set.

5 Carefully remove the flan tin and place the cheesecake on a serving plate.

6 Arrange the soft fruit on top of the cheesecake. Place the redcurrant jelly in a small bowl and add the hot water. Stir well until the jelly has melted. Leave it to cool and then spoon or lightly brush it over the fruit to serve.

PEACH and TOFU MELBA

A dessert created by the great chef Escoffier as a tribute to Dame Nellie Melba, the equally famous Australian soprano. Peach Melba has become one of the world's favourite desserts and is the inspiration for this fabulous dairy-free version. You do need to use fresh as opposed to canned peaches, as they lift it to a very special dish.

SERVES 4

4 peaches
30ml/2 tbsp caster (superfine) sugar
2 vanilla pods (beans)
raspberries, to decorate
60ml/4 tbsp soya yogurt, to serve

For the vanilla sauce
700g/1lb 6oz silken tofu
50g/2oz/½ cup icing (confectioners') sugar
105ml/7 tbsp apple juice
2 drops vanilla essence (extract)

For the raspberry sauce
300g/11oz/scant 2 cups fresh or
    frozen raspberries

2 Leave the peaches until they are cool enough to handle, then carefully peel off the skins with your fingers. If the skins do not come off easily, put the peaches back in the water and simmer for a further 2 minutes.

5 To make the raspberry sauce, put all but four of the raspberries in a food processor or blender and process until puréed. If you don't like the pips (seeds), then push the purée through a sieve with a spatula.

1 Place four wide, individual serving glasses in the freezer to chill. Meanwhile place the whole peaches in a pan and add just enough water to cover. Add the sugar and the vanilla pods. Bring to the boil, lower the heat and simmer gently for 10 minutes. Remove the peaches from the pan with a slotted spoon and set aside.

3 Cut the peaches in half and gently ease out the stone (pit). Set aside while you make the sauces.

6 Remove the glasses from the freezer and place two peach halves in the base of each glass, followed by some of the vanilla sauce. Drizzle over some of the raspberry sauce. Add a spoonful of soya yogurt and decorate with the reserved fresh raspberries before serving.

COOK'S TIPS
• The peaches do not have to be perfectly ripe because they are poached. If you can find them, white peaches look stunning.
• If the raspberries are a little sharp, stir 50–75g/2–3oz/½–¾ cup icing (confectioners') sugar into the sauce before spooning it over the desserts.
• You can process frozen raspberries without thawing them first, but the fruit for decoration must be thawed.

4 To make the vanilla sauce, put the tofu with the icing sugar in a food processor or blender and add the apple juice and vanilla essence. Process until smooth, then tip into a bowl and set aside in the refrigerator until required.

VARIATIONS
• Nectarines can be used instead of peaches, and if the fruit is perfectly ripe then do not worry about poaching it. Nectarines are also easier to peel.
• These sauces are also delicious with melon. Cut 2 small, well-chilled cantaloupe melons in half horizontally and scoop out the seeds with a spoon. Fill the cavities with vanilla sauce and fresh raspberries and top with the raspberry sauce. Omit the soya yogurt.

CHOCOLATE MOUSSE

All the richness and flavour of a traditional mousse, but with much less fat – you can have the best of both worlds. For a child-friendly version, omit the coffee and stir the grated rind of an orange into the melted chocolate mixture.

SERVES 6–8

60ml/4 tbsp golden (light
   corn) syrup
115g/4oz plain (semisweet) chocolate
   (preferably 70% cocoa solids), broken
   into pieces
15ml/1 tbsp instant coffee mixed with
   30ml/2 tbsp boiling water or
   30ml/2 tbsp very strong brewed
   coffee (optional)
350g/12oz silken tofu
2 eggs, separated
natural (plain) yogurt, to serve
cocoa powder (unsweetened),
   to decorate

1 Place the syrup, chocolate and coffee, if using, in a heatproof bowl set over a pan of simmering water until melted. Stir together, remove from the heat then leave to cool slightly.

2 Place the tofu and chocolate mixture in a food processor or blender and process for 1–2 minutes. Add the egg yolks and process to a thick cream. Transfer to a large bowl.

3 Whisk the egg whites in a clean, grease-free bowl until stiff, then gradually fold into the chocolate mixture, a little at a time, using a rubber spatula.

4 Spoon the mousse into serving glasses, pots or cups and chill in the refrigerator until set. Spoon a little yogurt on top of each mousse, sprinkle with cocoa powder, and serve.

BANANA and PECAN TOFU PIE

This variation of a classic American dessert is guaranteed to become a firm family favourite. The combination of crisp pastry, creamy vanilla-tofu custard, sweet banana and crunchy pecans glazed with maple syrup is absolutely irresistible.

SERVES 6

15g/½oz/1 tbsp cornflour (cornstarch)
25g/1oz/2 tbsp demerara (raw) sugar
175ml/6fl oz/¾ cup soya milk
175g/6oz silken tofu, drained
2.5ml/½ tsp vanilla essence (extract)
2 large ripe bananas
18cm/7in pre-baked pastry case (pie shell)
75g/3oz/¾ cup pecan nut halves
7.5ml/½ tbsp maple syrup or clear honey,
    to glaze

1 Put the cornflour and sugar in a pan and stir together. Add a little of the milk and combine into a smooth paste. Add the rest of the milk gradually, stirring between each addition.

2 Place the pan over a low heat and cook, stirring constantly, until the custard thickens, coating the back of the spoon.

3 Place the custard, tofu, vanilla essence and 1 banana in a blender or food processor and blend until smooth.

4 Slice the remaining bananas and arrange the slices over the base of the pre-baked pastry case. Spoon the tofu mixture on top and spread evenly. Decorate with the pecan nuts then glaze with the maple syrup. Chill the tart for 1 hour before serving.

CARROT CAKE with SILKEN TOFU FROSTING

Everybody loves this sweet, moist cake with its delicious creamy frosting. It makes a great dessert for family meals and when entertaining, and is also a tasty pick-me-up when you need a mid-morning coffee break – in the unlikely event of any being left over.

SERVES 8

90g/3½oz/7 tbsp soya margarine
5ml/1 tsp cardamom pods
225g/8oz/2 cups wholemeal (whole-wheat)
    or plain (all-purpose) flour
15ml/1 tbsp baking powder
130g/4½oz/⅔ cup demerara (raw) sugar
225g/8oz carrots, coarsely grated
50g/2oz/scant ½ cup sultanas
    (golden raisins)
5ml/1 tsp ground cinnamon
pinch of ground cloves
75ml/5 tbsp sunflower oil
2 eggs, lightly beaten

For the frosting
175g/6oz silken tofu
25g/1oz/¼ cup icing (confectioners') sugar
7.5ml/½ tbsp apple juice
drop of vanilla essence (extract)
finely grated rind of ½ orange

1 Preheat the oven to 160°C/325°F/ Gas 3. Grease and line an 18cm/7in loose-based cake tin (pan).

2 Melt the soya margarine in a small pan over a low heat, then leave to cool.

3 Remove the seeds from the cardamom pods, discarding the pods. Place the seeds in a mortar and crush with a pestle.

4 Mix the flour, baking powder, sugar, carrots, sultanas and all the spices together in a large bowl.

5 Add the margarine, oil and eggs and mix to a soft cake batter.

6 Spoon or pour the mixture into the prepared cake tin and smooth the top. Bake for 60–65 minutes, or until a skewer inserted into the centre comes out clean and the top is golden brown and firm to the touch.

7 Remove the cake from the oven and place, still in the tin, on a wire rack to cool completely. Carefully remove the cake from the tin and return to the wire rack for frosting.

8 Meanwhile, make the frosting by placing the tofu and icing sugar in a food processor or blender. Add the apple juice, vanilla and orange rind. Process the mixutre until smooth and creamy. Spoon the frosting over the top of the cake and spread with the back of a knife or spatula.

VARIATIONS
• Stir in 15ml/1 tbsp finely chopped walnuts instead of or as well as the sultanas (golden raisins) in step 4.
• Substitute the grated rind of 1 lemon for the orange rind in the frosting.
• For a really special frosting, flavour the icing (confectioners') sugar with fragrant edible leaves or petals, such as lemon balm or geranium leaves or rose petals. The night before, place the sugar in a small bowl. Tear 3–4 petals or leaves into medium pieces and stir into the sugar. Cover with clear film (plastic wrap) and leave overnight. Remove and discard the petals or leaves before mixing the sugar with the other ingredients.

INDEX